CITYSPOTS
MILAN

**Barbara Radcliffe Rogers
& Stillman Rogers**

Written by Barbara Radcliffe Rogers & Stillman Rogers
Updated by Kathryn Tomasetti and Tristan Rutherford

Published by Thomas Cook Publishing
A division of Thomas Cook Tour Operations Limited
Company registration No: 1450464 England
The Thomas Cook Business Park, 9 Coningsby Road
Peterborough PE3 8SB, United Kingdom
Email: books@thomascook.com, Tel: +44 (0)1733 416477
www.thomascookpublishing.com

Produced by The Content Works Ltd
Aston Court, Kingsmead Business Park, Frederick Place
High Wycombe, Bucks HP11 1LA
www.thecontentworks.com

Series design based on an original concept by Studio 183 Limited

ISBN: 978-1-84157-938-2

First edition © 2006 Thomas Cook Publishing
This second edition © 2008 Thomas Cook Publishing
Text © Thomas Cook Publishing
Maps © Thomas Cook Publishing/PCGraphics (UK) Limited
Transport map © Communicarta Limited

Series Editor: Kelly Anne Pipes
Project Editor: Linda Bass
Production/DTP: Steven Collins

Printed and bound in Spain by GraphyCems

Cover photography (Milan Duomo) © Shaun Egan/Getty Images

CONTENTS

SYMBOLS KEY

The following symbols are used throughout this book:

ⓐ address ☎ telephone ⓕ fax ⓦ website address
🕒 opening times Ⓝ public transport connections ⓘ important

The following symbols are used on the maps:

ℹ️ information office		▨ points of interest
✈ airport		O city
✚ hospital		O large town
🛡 police station		○ small town
🚌 bus station		▬ motorway
🚆 railway station		— main road
Ⓜ metro		— minor road
✝ cathedral		— railway
➊ numbers denote featured cafés & restaurants		

Hotels and restaurants are graded by approximate price as follows:
£ budget price ££ mid-range price £££ expensive

◗ *The impressive entrance to Galleria Vittorio Emanuele II*

INTRODUCING
Milan

Introduction

Milan is renowned for being a style-savvy, hip city, perhaps best known for its cutting-edge sense of fashion and attractive, well-dressed inhabitants. But it hides its inner self well, and, when you start to explore, you will discover numerous other wonders, including a surprising mix of architecture that puts art nouveau next to Gio Ponti and Renaissance splendour beside post-war, international style. Stop by a bar in the late afternoon and discover the spread of delicious snacks laid out for the nibbling. Simply take a detour past the designer shops of the Quadrilatero d'Oro or people-watch the preoccupied patrons of the Galleria shopping centre; peek into the tranquil green courtyards or listen to a street performer in the mellow Piazza Mercanti. You will soon discover that Milan has a sweet soul all of its own.

You do have to know where to look – head to the Navigli, where the young and hip Milanese spend their evenings at canal-side cafés and clubs. Surprises are tucked into churches (one is lined with human bones, another is only half the size it appears); museums (discover a powerful, unfinished work by Michelangelo); cemeteries; and even sprawling Parco Sempione (see page 77), where a dizzying tower with a hip café offers views as sweeping as those from the Duomo's rooftop.

Milan deserves a second look – and a third, and a fourth. Like the oyster, it may take a while to crack open the sometimes tough and unattractive shell, but the pearl inside is worth the effort.

● *Shopping heaven inside the Galleria*

When to go

For a better chance of sampling 'sunny Italy' in Milan, go between April and October. Take an umbrella, but expect balmy days and pleasant evenings. Real heat sets in by mid-July and, by August, becomes so oppressive that locals flee for the Mediterranean shore or the nearby lakes. Avoid August because all but the strictly tourist eateries (and much else in the city) are closed for the whole month. Although the weather is cooler around the lakes, hotels are packed with Milanese who've fled the sizzling streets.

Between November and March, a cool fog settles over the city, sometimes for several weeks at a time. But this is the season for Milan's arts, music, performance and cultural events, so don't discount it just because of a touch of *brutto tempo*, or bad weather.

SEASONS & CLIMATE
Milan's winter days in January and February tend to be very damp, and average temperatures range between -3°C (25°F) and 6°C (43°F). Summertime (July and August) is hot and humid, with the thermometer often hovering around 29°C (85°F). Spring and autumn are the best seasons to visit the city, as the weather is moderate (17°C/63°F), although April and October are normally also the rainiest months.

ANNUAL EVENTS
Milan just loves to throw on its (fashionable) party clothes and let rip, and, when it comes to a knees-up, studied cool soon gets the Milanese elbow.

January

Corteo dei Re Magi (Wise Men Processional) (6 Jan) A procession to celebrate the three wise men's journey departs from Piazza del Duomo and finishes in Piazza Sant'Eustorgio.

Milano Moda Uomo (Men's Fashion Week) The Italian fashion year kicks off with the autumn/winter men's collection.
Ⓦ www.cameramoda.com

February

Carnevale (Shrove Tuesday (Mardi Gras) until first Sat in Lent) A pre-Lent bash, with parades, floats and costumed folk wandering the streets around Piazza del Duomo.

Milano Moda Donna (Women's Fashion Week) Autumn/winter lines, this time for the ladies. Ⓦ www.cameramoda.com

March

Oggi Aperto Historic buildings and monuments open to the public on the third weekend of the month. Contact the tourist office (see page 150) for additional information.

Film Festival Internazionale di Milano (Milan International Independent Film Festival) A week-long festival honouring independent film-makers, at venues around the city. Ⓦ www.miff.it

MIArt Hit the Fiera for Milan's exuberant and colourful art fair.
Ⓦ www.miart.it

April

Naviglio Grande Flower Market The streets of the Navigli are laden with flowers as hundreds of florists congregate for this massive flower market. ⓐ Alzaia Naviglio Grande
Ⓦ www.navigliogrande.mi.it

Salone Internazionale del Mobile (International Furniture & Design Fair) The world's biggest design fair hits Milan as design studios premiere their latest creations. Expect the peak of chic. Ⓦ www.cosmit.it

May

Milano Cortili Aperti (Milan Open Courtyards) On a Sunday in mid-May, private residence courtyards open for public viewing. ⓐ Via S. Paolo 10 ⓣ (02) 7631 8634 Ⓦ www.cortiliaperti.com

June

Festival Internazionale Gay Lesbico e Queer Culture (Gay & Lesbian Film Festival) A celebrated week of international, pink-tinged films at Teatro Strehler. ⓐ Largo Greppi 1 ⓣ (02) 5748 0889 Ⓦ www.cinemagaylesbico.it Ⓜ Metro: 2 to Lanza

Sagra di San Christoforo (Festival of Saint Christopher) (3rd Sun in June) Not-so-saintly celebrations along the Naviglio canals, featuring decorated barges.

Milano d'Estate (Summer in Milan) (June–Aug) Sponsored public concerts in Parco Sempione.

September

Milano Film Festival Young and experimental film-makers from all over the world show their creations in the newly democratised medium. ⓣ (02) 713 613 Ⓦ www.milanofilmfestival.it

Milano Moda Donna (Women's Fashion Week) Cutting-edge women's styles for next spring and summer. Ⓦ www.cameramoda.com

October
Festival Milano Contemporary music, dance, theatre and classical renditions. 🆆 www.milanomusica.org

Milano City Marathon Athletes, amateurs and people dressed as tomatoes pound along Milan's streets. ☎ (02) 6282 8755 🆆 www.milanocitymarathon.it ❶ Month may vary

December
La Scala Opera (7 Dec) The winter opera season gets off to a top-C turvy start. ☎ (02) 861 827 🆆 www.teatroallascala.org

Festa di Sant'Ambrogio (Feast day of Saint Ambrose) A favourite local holiday on the weekend closest to 7 December. Street parties kick off in the 'Oh bej! Oh bej!' craft market (see page 95) around the Sant'Ambrogio church.

PUBLIC HOLIDAYS
Capodanno (New Year's Day) 1 Jan
La Befana (Epiphany) 6 Jan
Pasqua (Easter Sunday) 23 Mar 2008; 12 Apr 2009
Lunedi di Pasqua (Easter Monday) 24 Mar 2008; 13 Apr 2009
Festa della Liberazione (Liberation Day) 25 Apr
Festa del Lavoro (Labour Day) 1 May
Festa della Repubblica (Anniversary of the Republic) 2 June
Ferragosto (Feast of the Assumption) 15 Aug
Tutti Santi (All Saints' Day) 1 Nov
Festa di Sant'Ambrogio (Feast of Saint Ambrose) 7 Dec
Festa dell'Immacolata (Feast of the Immaculate Conception) 8 Dec
Natale (Christmas) 25 Dec

Fashion

Twice a year, in late February and again in late September,
everybody who's anybody in Fashion (with a capital F) descends on
Milan for Milano Moda Donna, Women's Fashion Week. In June and
mid-January, men have their turn with Milano Moda Uomo.

Dozens of Milan designers – the cream of the fashion houses –
send top fashion models out to strut their stuff on the catwalks.
It's the high point in the city's busy calendar of international design
exhibitions – furniture, food and technology are just a few of the
other major trade shows held here – and it sends shock waves
through the clothing industry that are felt from Tokyo to New York,
even (though grudgingly) in Paris.

The major houses have their own show venues, some in
stunningly revamped warehouses in the old industrial sectors,
while the rest await their moment in the spotlight at the big
Fiera di Milano (ⓦ www.fieramilano.it). Known simply as Fiera,
Milan's trade fair centre covers an enormous stretch of real
estate west of Parco Sempione.

The catch for casual travellers without connections to the fashion
industry is that you can't get into the shows without invitations.
This means real credentials, not just a note on the letterhead of
your hometown dress shop. The other downside is that hotel rooms
are booked for months ahead of these weeks.

So why come then? You can watch it on TV and read about it in
the fashion pages almost anywhere in the world, but you can't feel
the buzz that changes the whole atmosphere of Milan. Hard as
it is to believe, people dress even better than usual, and the clubs
and bars are filled with people associated with the shows, and
with others trying to get a look at them and what they are wearing.

The excitement spills over to fill Milan's streets, shops and restaurants with a new electricity.

Less buzz may accompany the twice-yearly men's fashion weeks, but those, too, change the city, as drop-dead gorgeous models hit town and Milanese men take extra time to choose their shirts and knot their neckties.

Just so you know, the **Four Seasons Hotel** (ⓐ Via Gesu 6/8 ⓘ (02) 770 88) is one of the pet digs for the international fashionistas. Any time of year, if you're anybody worth the sales clerks' attention, you simply have your designer-shop bags delivered to the concierge there. You don't even need to give a room number – he'll know who you are.

◖ *Gottex Swimwear is just one of the many famous brands on the Milan catwalk*

History

Turmoil has characterised Milan since Lombardy's earliest settlers decorated their caves with pictures of hunting exploits. In the 5th century BC, Celts turned up and built the first settlement. Enter the Roman legions, demolishing the Celts' defences and establishing Mediolanum in 222 BC. Celts and Romans slugged it out until the Second Punic War brought Hannibal into the Po Valley from Spain. He knocked Roman heads together until he was sent packing. Then Mediolanum prospered in peace, growing in influence until it was made capital of Rome's 11th region in 15 BC.

By the third century AD, Milan had become the power centre of the western Roman empires. When Emperor Constantine gained control of the peninsula he recognised Christianity and ended persecution with the Edict of Milan in 313.

Bad times followed. Attila the Hun destroyed Milan in the 5th century, then, in 539, the Goths destroyed it again. Charlemagne engulfed it in 774, and by 1000 the town was controlled by bishops. In 1045 the city threw them off and became a commune, leading to years of conflict with nearby city-states. It was incorporated into the Holy Roman Empire in 1162, when it was again razed.

Various powerful families fought for control until 1450 when Francesco Sforza assumed control. The Sforza family ruled until 1535, when the Austrian Prince Philip took over. When he became King of Spain, Milan passed to Spanish control until 1706, when the Austrians reclaimed it.

Next, enter Napoleon: seen as a liberator by Milanese chafing under Austrian rule, he was welcomed by most, and the Austrians bowed out. In 1805 Napoleon created the Kingdom of Italy in French-controlled areas, crowning himself King in the Duomo, with Milan as his capital. When his fortunes reversed, Austria once again took the reins in 1815, but, feeling the muscle of their booming industry, manufacturing and commerce, in 1848 Milan's citizens rose against the Austrians – the beginning of the Risorgimento – and liberated the city. The new republic only lasted five months before it was defeated, but the city was freed by the entry of Victor Emmanuel's forces in 1859, when the new united Italy was born.

Dynamic growth continued, and Milan styled itself as Italy's cultural and economic capital. It was partly to protect its manufacturing edge from labour unrest that Milan backed Mussolini in his rise. But by 1945 Milan was ready to move on, and rose against the occupying Nazis, liberating the city in just three days. Largely destroyed by World War II bombing, Milan was quickly rebuilt, and its hard-working population set about making it Italy's de facto capital. In the post-war boom, Milan led Italy from a quaint backwater to a major industrial nation. But recent history hasn't all been a nonchalant vogue down the catwalk for the city, and the last three decades of the 20th century were particularly challenging, with Milan enduring the activities of the Red Brigade terrorist group and constant allegations of corruption among the city's politicians. Those difficulties have been overcome now and, as the first decade of the 21st century draws to a close, Milan is the industrial, commercial, political, intellectual, design and fashion capital of Italy. The government may be in Rome, but the power is where the money (and the stock market) is – in Milan.

Lifestyle

Fashion and style are at the heart of Milan's modus operandi. Walk down any street and you can easily distinguish the locals from the tourists. Local men are in suits so well tailored that they might have been sprayed on. And as for the women, no woman in Milan would run to the corner shop for toothpaste without first applying her full makeup and doing her hair.

Looks really do matter here, but it's not all about puffery and show; the outlook is more derived from a sense of style that starts being absorbed at birth. It goes beyond clothes to architecture, home décor, even to the feel of a pen or keyboard. Chic is everywhere. Whether it's a revolutionary building by architect Gio Ponti or the latest lemon-squeezer from Alessi, it will have serious class.

The Milanese stand out even in Italy for their finely tuned aesthetic perceptions, so it is not surprising that this influences the way they live. They dine out often and appreciate fine food. They are passionate about the opera, support artists and performers, and in general live the good life.

The Milanese are sometimes criticised by other Italians, especially those from the south, for their allegedly dour, nose-to-the-grindstone behaviour, but these same regions are glad for the financial support that hard-working Milan's success brings to the general welfare of Italy. If the Milanese play hard, dress stylishly, dine well and furnish their homes elegantly, it is because they have earned the right. And, for all the importance they attach to high fashion and the good life, they are hospitable, helpful and friendly to visitors. Just join them in a bar after work or on a Saturday evening in the Navigli and you won't see dour or buttoned-down – you'll see people who play as enthusiastically as they work.

Underneath all the style there is serious substance. Milan is a primarily Catholic city, although for most people this means going to mass only at Christmas and Easter. But the sensibility – the sense of drama and occasion – is there.

Milan is a fairly expensive city to live in. Yet, although rents tend to be high, it's very possible to get out and around town on very little. Public transport is economical, and food and drink cost much less than in France or the UK.

⬤ *Join locals for an aperitivo at Zucca*

Culture

Milan's artistic and musical heritage is a long and rich one. Important and influential Milanese people have supported arts and artists with commissions and left important cultural legacies to the city: four of the city's five significant art museums are based on private collections, and it was the patronage of the Sforza family that brought Leonardo da Vinci and the Renaissance architect Bramante to Milan.

The Milanese continue this tradition by supporting contemporary artists. The Triennale's (see page 76) purpose is to encourage and recognise good design and other major museums are dedicated to contemporary art. Milan's city-owned museums, including a portion of the outstanding collections in the Castello Sforzesco (see page 74), are free.

La Scala (see page 63) is, quite simply, the centre of the opera universe. Opera is popular with all ages and all classes of Italians, who consider it their national music. La Scala's opening night (see page 73) is the highlight of the social season, and good seats for major performances are difficult to get at any time.

It's not all classical and fine arts. Milan is the centre of the Italian music industry, with most major labels based here, and many famous bods live in Milan as a result. A little-known venue where recording artists perform selections from their latest albums to smaller audiences is the centrally located Teatro Manzoni (see page 73).

Concerts, whether Sunday morning jazz at Teatro Manzoni or a quartet playing chamber music at Teatro Dal Verme (see page 87), are well attended. See Entertainment & nightlife, page 28, for

● *Culture is everywhere – don't forget to look up!*

popular venues. The city's two primary classical and semi-classical performance ensembles are:

Filarmonica della Scala

The Philharmonic performs at Teatro alla Scala (see page 73), with tickets starting at €5, available at the theatre or on-line. ⓐ Piazza della Scala ⓣ (02) 7200 3744 ⓦ www.filarmonica.it ⓝ Metro: 1 to Duomo or Cordusio, 3 to Duomo, Montenapoleone; bus: 61; tram: 1, 2

Orchestra Sinfonica di Milano Giuseppe Verdi

About 50 concerts are performed each season, most Thursday and Friday evenings and Sunday afternoons. Tickets are sold at the Auditorium itself, at the tourist office (see page 150) and on-line, where the full programme is also available. ⓐ Auditorium di Milano, Largo Gustav Mahler ⓣ (02) 8338 9401 ⓦ www.orchestrasinfonica.milano.it ⓛ 14.30–19.00 Mon–Fri, closed Sat & Sun ⓝ Bus: 59, 71, 90, 91; tram: 3, 9, 15, 29, 30

▶ *The Duomo's ethereal sculptures and gothic architecture*

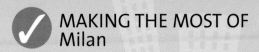

MAKING THE MOST OF
Milan

Shopping

Although it would be almost unthinkable to visit Milan and not at least walk through the Quadrilatero della Moda – the fashion quarter – few visitors actually shop there. Why? First, the prices are absurd. Second, so are many of the clothes. But it's endlessly entertaining to observe.

Cut-price designer fashions are sold in the outlets and consignment shops, where you'll see overstocks, last season's line, and items that have been worn by models. Discounts on these are usually 50 per cent to 70 per cent of the original tag. For more affordable clothes that still reflect the *Milano* look, shop along Corso Buenos Aires or Via Torino or in the galleries off Corso Vittorio Emanuele II. Most stores are open 15.30–19.30 Monday, and 09.30–19.30 Tuesday to Saturday. Smaller shops are generally open 09.30–12.30 and 15.30–19.30, often closing for *pausa pranzo*, or a lunchtime break.

Street markets are fun to browse, and they can turn up some surprises, such as previously owned designer clothes for a few euros. A very popular one is on Tuesday and Saturday morning at Viale Papiniano (see page 95). Milan has a full schedule of street markets, listed in the free newspaper *Hello Milano* (Ⓦ www.hellomilano.it).

Shows by craftspeople are a good source of one-offs. These, like artisans' workshops and studios, allow visitors the added opportunity of meeting the craftspeople and watching them at work. Every Saturday, **Fiera di Senigallia**, held along the Darsena, mixes original handicrafts with other items, new and used (Ⓐ Viale d'Annunzio Ⓛ 08.00–18.00).

For antiques and collectables, try the **Mercato dell'Antiquariato di Brera** (Ⓐ Via Fiori Chiari Ⓛ 09.00–18.00), where you'll find antiques, old books and jewellery on the third Saturday of every

month. Hit the massive Mercatone dell'Antiquariato on the
Naviglio Grande Canal (last Sunday of each month) and the
market at Piazza Diaz (last Saturday of each month) which also
has antiques.

USEFUL SHOPPING PHRASES

What time do the shops open/close?
A che ora aprono/chiudono i negozi?
Ah keh ohrah ahprohnoh/kewdohnoh ee nehgotsee?

How much is this?
Quanto costa questo?
Kwantoh kostah kwestoh?

Can I try this on?
Posso provarlo?
Pohsoh prohvarloh?

My size is ...
La mia taglia è ...
Lah meeyah tahlyah eh ...

I'll take this one, thank you
Prenderò questo, grazie
Prehndehroh kwestoh, grahtsyeh

Can you show me the one in the window/this one?
Può mostrarmi quello in vetrina/questo?
Poh mohstrahrmee kwehloh een vehtreenah/kwestoh?

This is too large/too small/too expensive
Questo è troppo grande/troppo piccolo/troppo caro
*Kwestoh eh trohpoh grahndeh/ trohpoh peekohloh/
trohpoh kahroh*

Eating & drinking

Some of Italy's top chefs work in Milan, and locals support them by dining out often, so the food scene is as fast-paced as the fashion one. But, as in any city, you can find outstanding, mediocre and inferior food, depending on where you look.

Travellers expecting the stereotypical Italian red-sauce-on-spaghetti may be surprised in Milan. While tomato-based sauces are found, Milanese cooking includes a wide array of dishes, and rice is as likely to be offered as pasta. In fact, perhaps the most classic of all northern Italian dishes is *risotto Milanese*, a dreamy-creamy rice dish made with saffron-infused broth – variations incorporate *porcini* mushrooms, shellfish or other ingredients.

Italians call their eating-places by a bewildering variety of names, and the lines between them blur. A *trattoria* usually has a more limited and less pricey menu than a *ristorante*, occasionally with a chalkboard list of choices. An *osteria* is supposedly a wine bar that serves snacks and sometimes a few dishes (think pub, Italian-style), but could in practice be a chi-chi 'rustic' country inn. A *pizzeria* is usually a full restaurant that specialises in wood-oven pizza, but it might also be a place that serves only pizza. For home-style cooking, look for signs advertising *cucina casalinga* and for a sandwich or quick lunch, go to a bar or café.

PRICE CATEGORIES
Prices are per person, for an average three-course meal, excluding wine.
£ up to €30   ££ €30–50   £££ over €50

COUNTING EUROS

Food – and the social milieu of dining out – is a major part of the Italian experience, but it can be a pricey one. Quality is often – although not always – matched with high prices that can equal those of Rome or Venice.

One euro-stretching strategy is to shop at markets, such as the daily ones found at *mercati comunali* (try the one on Viale Umbria 🕐 09.00–13.00, 15.00–19.00), covered markets scattered throughout the city. Pick up picnic ingredients (cheese, local salami and breads are always available) and carry them to **Giardini Pubblici** (Ⓜ Metro: Palestro; bus: 94) for an urban picnic.

If breakfast is not included in your room rate, don't despair: cafés and bars are much better value than hotels. Coffee with hot milk – cappuccino or caffè latte – is drunk only at breakfast. Coffee ordered at any other time of day will automatically be espresso unless you request otherwise. In Italy, a bar is not just for alcoholic drinks; it's the place to go for a quick cup of coffee or a snack, too.

A typical menu will be divided into courses: *antipasti* (starters), *primi* (first course), *secondi* (second course) and *dolci* (pudding). Not all Italians order all four, and neither should you, unless you are very hungry. Vegetables are not usually served with the main dish; order them from the *contorni* list.

Local specialities, along with *risotto Milanese*, include *cotoletta Milanese*, a breaded veal cutlet similar to *Wiener schnitzel*, and *osso bucco* – a tasty dish of slowly braised veal shanks and bone

● *Feast your eyes and your taste buds in a* gelateria

marrow in a rich tomato and wine sauce, sprinkled with garlic
and citrus zest.

Wine bars give you a chance to sample by the glass without
committing to a bottle. Look for the dry red Botticino and Cellatica,
as well as the sparkling Franciacorte. Even in neighbourhood
trattorie, the *vino di tavola* served by the carafe is almost certain
to be very drinkable.

The Milanese dine late by northern European standards, and
most restaurants don't open for dinner until 19.30 or 20.00. Lunch
is served from 12.30 until 14.30. Select a spot for your evening meal
and book a table (or ask your hotel to do it). It is especially important
to book ahead – at least a day or two – for popular restaurants on
Friday and Saturday evenings.

Many restaurants close on Sunday or Monday, and in August,

when the whole city seems to move to the lakes or sea; at these times you may have trouble finding any eating places open.

In most restaurants you can pay by credit card, although smaller *osterie* and *trattorie* may only accept cash. Tipping is appreciated, but is not a fixed amount. A 10 per cent tip is considered generous; €2–€5 is a respectable amount, and a 20-cent tip is usually added at a bar. Upmarket restaurants may add a service charge, which should be noted on the bill, in which case no further tip is expected.

USEFUL DINING PHRASES

I would like a table for ... people
Vorrei un tavolo per ... persone
Vohray oon tavohloh pehr... pehrsohneh

Excuse me!
Scusi!
Skoozhee!

May I have the bill, please?
Mi dà il conto, per favore?
Mee dah eel cohntoh pehr fahvohreh?

Could I have it well-cooked/medium/rare please?
Potrei averlo ben cotto/mediamente cotto/ al sangue, per favore?
Pohtray ahvehrloh behn kohtoh/ mehdyahmehnteh kohtoh/ ahl sahngweh, pehr fahvohreh?

I am a vegetarian. Does this contain meat?
Sono vegetariano/vegetariana (fem.). Contiene carne?
*Sohnoh vehjehtehrehahnoh/vehjehtehrehahnah.
Kontyehneh kahrneh?*

Entertainment & nightlife

Highbrow, lowbrow, club scene, grand funk, grand opera, drag shows, chamber music, grunge, jazz, Afro-pop, original-language theatre, international celebrity performances, street mimes, movie premieres, underground bands – if it's entertaining, it'll be in Milan.

The free publications *Hello Milano* (Ⓦ www.hellomilano.it) and *Easy Milano* (Ⓦ www.easymilano.it), both available at the tourist office, have complete listings for all the major and minor venues. For what's on at clubs and at smaller and alternative venues, look for *Zero Due*, a fortnightly free booklet available in some cafés and bars.

For many clubs, the music and vibe – and thus the clientele – change by the night of the week, so it may be rock 'n' roll at Alcatraz (see page 86) on Saturday, but strictly for teenagers at Magazzini Generali (see page 72).

If you're not well dressed, you may be turned away. This is not true everywhere, but the smarter the club's clientele, the more likely the bouncer is to keep it that way. Just remember that you can't soar with the eagles if you dress like a turkey.

Some clubs give you a card as you enter, which is punched at the coatroom and for every drink, then you pay as you leave. Admission charges, which range from €10–€20, may include one drink. At clubs all drinks – hard or soft – are usually the same price. Clubs are empty until near midnight, at which point they quickly fill, and remain open until around 04.00. Most are closed in July and August.

The major international acts go to one of the three big entertainment venues: Alcatraz (see page 86); **DatchForum** is the most important venue for catching international superstars such as David Bowie, Shakira, Justin Timberlake and the like (ⓐ Via G Di Vittorio 6,

Assago ☎ 199 128 800 Ⓦ www.forumnet.it Ⓜ shuttle bus provided from metro: 2 to Famagosta); Magazzini Generali (see page 72). For tickets, go to a booking centre in one of the major music stores – the most centrally located is **Messaggerie Musicali** (Ⓐ Corso Vittorio Emanuele II ☎ (02) 760 551 Ⓦ www.messaggeriemusicali.it) – or on-line, from **Ticket One** (Ⓦ www.ticketone.it) or **BarleyArts** (Ⓦ www.barleyarts.it).

🔵 Big name bands rock Alcatraz during the week and DJs play at weekends

Sport & relaxation

Though not technically a religion, football ranks up there with oxygen when it comes to a lot of Milanese people's necessities for life. Indeed, all sports are engaged in or viewed with impressive zeal here. It's not the taking part that counts – it's the winning.

SPECTATOR SPORTS

Milan is home to two major football teams that use the same stadium, Stadio Giuseppe Meazza (San Siro Stadium, see page 92). AC Milan and Inter provide the fierce rivalry that divides the city twice a year, when they clash at their shared stadium in the San Siro district. Tickets are pricey, and the crowd is rowdy – but these derby matches are unmissable.

Tickets for AC Milan are available at ❷ New Milan Point, Corso San Gottardo 2 ❶ (02) 8942 2711 ❶ 10.00–19.30 Mon–Sat, closed Sun. For Inter tickets, go to ❸ Box office, Feltrinelli Books & Music, Piazza Piemonte 2 ❶ (02) 433 541 ❶ 11.00–14.30, 15.30–19.00 Mon–Sat, closed Sun. Alternatively, purchase tickets on-line at ⓦ www.acmilan.com or ⓦ www.inter.it. Be aware that all tickets are issued in the individual purchaser's name (think airline tickets) and ID is needed upon entry. If you take someone else's ticket, be sure to fill out a transfer form, found on each team's website.

PARTICIPATION SPORTS

With the lakes and mountains so close, most outdoor sports enthusiasts head north. Lakeside sports centres offer equipment rental, and hiking guides and maps are available at tourist offices (especially for trails around Lake Como). With so many mountains, there is a lot of territory to explore on mountain bikes.

🔺 *Why not visit the Meazza Stadium?*

Boats of all sorts are available on the lakes. Ask for *barca* (boat), *barca a vela* (sailing boat) or *motoscafo* (motorboat). Put these together with *noleggio* (for hire) and you're rocking and rolling. To swim, look for small *piscina* (swimming pool) or *spiaggia* (beach) signs along the lakeshores, but don't expect broad sandy beaches. Most are stony or made of gravel, so you will need a blanket or heavy towel.

Golf
Lombardy has 35 nine- or eighteen-hole courses, nine promotional courses and nine practice locations. Most open all year, so golfers should be happy either in the city or around the lakes. Be sure to call ahead for guest status and to reserve a time.

Milan South Golf Club Le Rovedine, 18 holes, par 72, only 4 km (2 1/2 miles) from Milan. ⓐ Via Karl Marx 18, Noverasco di Opera ⓘ (0257) 606 420 Ⓦ www.rovedine.com Ⓛ Tues–Sun, closed Mon

Milan North Golf Club Milano, in Monza, has an 18-hole and a 9-hole course, par 72/36, 18 km (11 miles) from Milan. ❸ Via Mulini San Giorgio 7, Parco di Monza ❸ (039) 303 081 ❤ www.golfclubmilano.it ❸ Tues–Sun, closed Mon

⬥ *Sailing on Lake Como*

Milan East Molinetto Country Club is an 18-hole, par 71 course, 10 km (6 miles) from Milan. ⓐ Strada Statale Padana Superiore 11, Cernusco Sul Naviglio ⓣ (0292) 105 128
ⓦ www.molinettocountryclub.it ⓛ Tues–Sun, closed Mon
Milan West Green Club Lainate, 18 holes, par 71, 10 km (6 miles) from Milan. ⓐ Via A Manzoni 45, Lainate ⓣ (0293) 710 76
ⓦ www.greenclubgolf.it ⓛ 08.00–21.00
Lake Como Golf Club Villa d'Este has an 18-hole course and is among Europe's most challenging par 69 courses, 7 km (4 miles) from Como. ⓐ Via per Cantu 13, Montorofano ⓣ (031) 200 200
ⓦ www.villadeste.it ⓛ Wed–Mon, Mar–Dec, closed Tues, Jan & Feb

Horse Riding

Centro Ippico Tenuta la Torre All levels of riders are welcome here, and there are English-speaking guides for trips into the hills and mountains around Lake Como. ⓐ Follow yellow signs between Menaggio and Porlezza ⓣ (338) 894 7814 ⓦ www.menaggio.com
ⓝ Bus: line C12
Circolo Ippico Il Grillo A 13th-century farm near Como offers rides around tiny Lake Montorfano. The trips last from an hour to a full day and are offered at all levels of difficulty. ⓐ Via Chigollo 7, Capiago Intimiano ⓣ (031) 462 219 ⓦ www.grillo-como.it
English and Western saddles are available at both places.

RELAXATION

Fitness has become very popular with the Milanese, and health clubs are everywhere, so you can pump iron, tread water, steam yourself and be expertly kneaded almost on call. You'll want to be wearing the latest in work-out wear, of course.

Accommodation

Style-savvy Milan has some of Italy's classiest lodgings, from *belle époque* classics to the edgiest new art hotels. It also has a few of those charming, small family-run inns that are more often associated with the lakes.

The various Italian names for 'hotel' can be puzzling, and it's much better simply to go by description and the size. Don't be surprised to find many small city hotels on upper floors of business buildings, with no ground-floor lobby. These are often quite nice, and tend to be less costly than those with spacious public areas. Italy's star system helps you know what to expect of various lodging levels, and is based on regular inspections. For example, 2-star hotels will have private bathrooms; 3-star will have in-room telephones and television.

Establish the rate when booking (ask for special packages, especially on weekends, which can bring the most outrageous Milan rates down to reasonable), and request fax or email confirmation. Be sure to book well in advance for popular periods such as Easter week and during August around the lakes (incidentally, Milan is nearly empty then).

HOTELS

Campeggio Citta di Milano £ A wooded campground offering sites for tents, air-conditioned double rooms and 30 bungalows, which sleep

PRICE CATEGORIES
Prices are for double rooms, per night, not including breakfast.
£ up to €85   **££** €85–150   **£££** over €150

up to six people each. ⓐ Via Gaetano Airaghi 61 ⓣ (02) 4820 7017
ⓕ (02) 4820 2999 ⓦ www.campingmilano.it ⓝ Metro: 1 to De Angeli,
then bus: 72

Hotel Cavalieri della Corona £ The perfect choice for your last night
in town if you're returning a rented car to Malpensa – or just to
avoid last-minute hassles. Located in a nearby village, it has a pool,
dining and free shuttle connections to the airport. ⓐ Via Baroldo 12,
Cardano al Campo (Varese) ⓣ (0331) 730 350 ⓕ (0331) 730 348
ⓦ www.bestwestern.it

Hotel Del Sole £ Small but well-located hotel with clean and
comfortable, if simply furnished, rooms. The attractive breakfast
room is accessed by a spiral staircase. ⓐ Via Gaspare Spontini 6
ⓣ (02) 2951 2971 ⓕ (02) 2951 3689 ⓦ delsole.hotelsinmilan.it
ⓝ Metro: 2 to Lima

Hotel Sanpi Milano £ Close to the Stazione Centrale but in a safe
neighbourhood, this recently renovated hotel has individually
designed rooms featuring upscale décor and all expected amenities.
A patio makes you forget you're in a city. ⓐ Via Lazzaro Palazzi 18
ⓣ (02) 2951 3341 ⓕ (02) 2940 2451 ⓦ www.hotelsanpimilano.it
ⓝ Metro: 2, 3 to Stazione Centrale

Nettuno £ Far from posh, but gloriously atmospheric and friendly.
Handy for the whole city, very comfortable and with staff who
should be filed under w, for 'warm', 'welcoming' and, yes, 'wonderful'.
ⓐ Via Tadino 27 ⓣ (02) 2940 4481 ⓦ www.nettunomilano.it
ⓝ Metro: 1 to Porta Venezia; bus: 60

Ostello Piro Rotta £ Rare Milan hostel quarters are in the vicinity of the Fiera. Go during April, September or October to take advantage of the good-value bed & breakfast rate. ⓐ Viale Salmoiraghi 1 ⓣ (02) 3926 7095 ⓕ (02) 3300 0191 ⓦ www.ostellionline.org ⓒ Closed 23 Dec–13 Jan ⓜ Metro: 1 to QT8; bus: 68, 90, 91

Hotel Gelsomina £–££ A ten-room hotel with bright, cosy rooms, private baths, TV and high-speed internet. Located on the north side of the city centre, near the Fiera. ⓐ Via Piero della Francesca 4/7 ⓣ (02) 3491 742 ⓕ (02) 3180 1413 ⓦ www.hotelgelsomina.it ⓜ Bus: 43, 57, 169; tram: 11

⬤ *Combine business and relaxation in the Chedi's swish environs*

Best Western Hotel Felice Casati ££ All spruced up and shining after a complete renovation, this hotel ticks all the necessary boxes, and then some. Fabulous location. 🚇 Via Felice Casati 18 ☎ (02) 2940 4208 📠 (02) 2940 4618 🌐 www.bestwestern.it Ⓜ Metro: 1 to Porta Venezia; bus: 60

Grand Hotel Verdi ££ Close to the hip Brera district, the Verdi plays on the operatic theme with dramatic stage-set décor. You could stage an opera in any of the huge guest rooms. 🚇 Via Melchiorre Gioia 6 ☎ (02) 62 371 🌐 www.grandhotelverdi.com Ⓜ Metro: 3 to Montenapoleone; tram: 1, 2

Hotel London ££ A very well-priced hotel, considering its unbeatable central location and the excellent services offered. 🚇 Via Rovello 3 ☎ (02) 7202 0166 📠 (02) 8057 037 🌐 www.hotel-london-milan.com Ⓜ Metro: 1 to Cairoli

Antica Locanda Leonardo ££–£££ Rooms are a pretty combination of traditional charm and modern comforts; service is exceptionally friendly. 🚇 Corso Magenta 78 ☎ (02) 4801 4197 📠 (02) 4801 9012 🌐 www.anticalocandaleonardo.com Ⓜ Metro: 1, 2 to Cadorna; tram: 16, 18

The Chedi ££–£££ The first European hotel for chic hoteliers GHM, The Chedi offers cutting-edge technology within Asian, zen-like décor. While slightly out of the city centre, the location is superb for business travellers. 🚇 Via Villapizzone 24 ☎ (02) 3631 888 📠 (02) 3631 870 🌐 www.hotel-milano-the-chedi.com Ⓜ Bus: 57; tram: 1, 12

First Hotel Malpensa ££–£££ For morning departures, a room at the airport saves endless hassles, especially at this family-owned, modern hotel. Rooms are tech-ed up and soundproofed, and free shuttles whisk guests off to their departure terminals. ⓐ Via Baracca 34, Case Nuove, Somma Lombardo, Varese ⓣ (0331) 717 045 ⓕ (0331) 230 827 ⓦ www.firsthotel.it

Hotel Ariston ££–£££ A modern and ecologically oriented hotel, the Ariston is located at the end of Via Torino, minutes from the buzzing Navigli area. ⓐ Largo Carrobbio 2 ⓣ (02) 7200 0556 ⓕ (02) 7200 0914 ⓦ www.brerahotels.com/ariston ⓜ Metro: 2 to Sant'Ambrogio; tram: 2, 3, 14

Hotel Gran Duca di York ££–£££ With its sunny rooms in the centre of the city, this small, well-kept hotel is an ideal base, close to the Duomo and Via Torino. ⓐ Via Moneta 1A ⓣ (02) 874 863 ⓕ (02) 869 0344 ⓦ www.ducadiyork.com ⓜ Metro: 1, 3 to Duomo; tram: 1, 2, 3, 12, 14, 16, 27

Hotel Mediolanum ££–£££ Well positioned, near the train station, Porta Venezia and Piazza Repubblica, this hotel is modern and comfortable, and has in-room internet connections and Wi-Fi, and nearby fitness facilities. If you request it in advance, the hotel will book your visit to Da Vinci's *Last Supper*. ⓐ Via Mauro Macchi 1 (at Via Napo Torriani) ⓣ (02) 6705 312 ⓕ (02) 6698 1921 ⓦ www.mediolanumhotel.com ⓜ Metro: 3 to Stazione Centrale or Repubblica

3 Rooms £££ Indulge yourself with a stay at one of these three sizeable apartments, each furnished with a mix of modern and antique furniture. With immediate access to Corso Como 10's bar, restaurant, garden, bookstore and exhibition space, these gems are sometimes booked up months in advance. ⓐ Corso Como 10

ℹ (02) 626 163 🆆 www.3rooms-
10corsocomo.com
Ⓜ Metro: 2 to Garibaldi

Grand Hotel et de Milan £££
Oozing elegant charm,
this traditional hotel was
constructed in 1863. A favourite
of Hemingway and home to
Giuseppe Verdi for almost
30 years, the Grand Hotel is just
off chic Via Montenapoleone,
and a short walk from La Scala.

🔺 *Hotel Gran Duca di York*

🅐 Via Manzoni 29 ℹ (02) 723 141
ℹ (02) 8646 0861 🆆 www.grandhoteletdemilan.it Ⓜ Metro: 3 to
Montenapoleone; tram: 1, 2

The Gray £££ Just steps from Piazza del Duomo, this boutique hotel
is a mix of avant-garde design and elegant sophistication. Linger over
the diferent room options – each one differs dramatically, and guests
can take their pick of duplexes, jacuzzis or a terrace with a view.
Gorgeous. 🅐 Via San Raffaele 6 ℹ (02) 720 8951 ℹ (02) 866 526
🆆 www.hotelthegray.com Ⓜ Metro: 1, 3 to Duomo

The Straf £££ A surprising blend of comfort and punkish industrial
design, the Straf boasts an excellent position just behind the
Galleria. Don't let the 18th-century façade fool you – behind it,
rooms are decked out in polished concrete and burnished copper.
🅐 Via San Raffaele 3 ℹ (02) 805 081 ℹ (02) 8909 5294
🆆 www.straf.it Ⓜ Metro: 1, 3 to Duomo

THE BEST OF MILAN

As Milan is nice and compact, you'll have no trouble fitting in a flit to all of its most magnetic attractions.

TOP 10 ATTRACTIONS

- **The Duomo** Italy's towering tribute to Gothic architecture – climb to the rooftop for dizzying views over the Milan skyline (see page 60)

- **Fashion Weeks** Beautiful people in beatiful clothes that show why the city is still synonymous with what matters in fashion (see page 12)

- **Galleria Vittorio Emanuele II** Wander through Italy's original shopping centre, or stop for a drink at one of the many pavement cafés, and watch the world stroll by (see page 60)

- **Sant'Ambrogio** After the Duomo, Sant'Ambrogio is considered to be Milan's most significant church, with 16 centuries of architecture etched upon it (see page 90)

○ *The imposing Castello Sforzesco in central Milan*

- ***The Last Supper*** A trip to Milan would not be complete without a visit to one of the world's most famous paintings, found at Santa Maria delle Grazie (see page 77)

- **Quadrilatero della Moda (Fashion Quarter)** An entire district of fashionista nirvana, including Via Montenapoleone, Via della Spiga, Via Manzoni and Via Sant'Andrea (see page 62)

- **Castello Sforzesco** Home to a number of manageable museums, the Castello Sforzesco and surrounding Parco Sempione are appealing for all ages (see page 74)

- **Palazzo Bagatti Valsecchi** Step back in time, into Italy's illustrious Renaissance past, with a wander through this perfect palace (see page 64)

- **Navigli nightlife** Spend an evening in and around Milan's canals, taking advantage of the hip nightlife (see page 98)

- **La Brera neighbourhood** Packed with vibrant bars and trendy *trattorias*, this characteristic neighbourhood is a unique spot in the city at any time of day (see page 74)

Suggested itineraries

HALF-DAY: MILAN IN A HURRY

Visit the Duomo (see page 60), including the rooftop – if it's a clear day, you can see all the way to the Alps. Then wander into Milan's favourite people-watching place, Galleria Vittorio Emanuele II, to window shop and stop for an expensive coffee or *aperitivo* at Zucca (see page 70), a timeless café where moneyed locals meet. Go all the way through the Galleria to Piazza della Scalla, then head to the last bit of medieval Milan, Piazza Mercanti.

1 DAY: TIME TO SEE A LITTLE MORE

After the Duomo and its neighbours, stroll up Via Manzoni, stopping to look into one of the hidden gardens behind the buildings to your right, and into the Quadrilatero della Moda. The Palazzo Bagatti Valsecchi Renaissance art museum (see page 64) is in the middle of this district, a refreshing step back after you've seen more than your fill of the latest designer wear. Or head for Santa Maria delle Grazie to see Da Vinci's *The Last Supper* (see page 77), then continue on to the city's most historic church, Sant'Ambrogio (see page 90). By then it should be time for an *aperitivo* at **Baci & Abbracci** (🅐 Via E de Amicis 44 🕐 (02) 8901 3605 🅦 www.bacieabbraci.it), just down the road, where the (extremely) beautiful people hang out. For the evening, choose between the lively Brera's restaurants or the canalside Navigli's hip nightlife.

2–3 DAYS: TIME TO SEE MUCH MORE

With a little more time, you can take in Castello Sforzesco (see page 74), peeking into its museums to see Michelangelo's last unfinished work, the *Rondanini Pietà*. Behind the castle is Parco Sempione (see page 77).

There, take a trip to the top of the Gio Ponte tower for a 360-degree view, then stop for a break in the classy Cavalli café below. Visit the latest design exhibit at the nearby Triennale, also in the park. If *The Last Supper* inspired you to learn more about Da Vinci – or if scientific stuff fascinates you – head for the Museo Nazionale della Scienza e della Tecnologia Leonardo da Vinci (National Museum of Science and Technology, see page 94) to see the artist's inventions, or play with science using the interactive exhibits.

LONGER: ENJOYING MILAN TO THE FULL

After you've seen the sights of the city, do as the Romans did (and the Milanese do), and decamp to the lakes. Even in the winter, the weather is milder there, especially on Como's Tremezzina Riviera (see page 116) on the western shore. From spring until autumn, the gardens will be beautiful (they are even green in the winter) and a variety of lake ferries provide cheap cruises. If you long for nightlife, stay in Como (see page 102), the lake's largest town and a 40-minute train ride from Milan. Or choose the more peaceful Lake Maggiore (see page 120), generally favoured by a somewhat older crowd, but filled with activities and sights such as the Isole Borromeo (Borromean Islands, see page 134) with their palaces, gardens and mountain views.

◯ *Lakeside villa on Lake Como*

Something for nothing

Milan, no matter how you measure it, is an expensive city to visit, but it is an economical one to see. Not only are nearly all the churches free, with their own treasures of art and architecture to offer, but so are most of the city-owned museums.

The entirety of the castle, Castello Sforzesco (see page 74), is filled with treasures, and along with the must-see highlights, such as Michelangelo's *Rondanini Pietà*, gallery after gallery displays far

○ *Admire Milan's magnificent Duomo for free*

more than paintings and sculpture. The entire museum of practical and decorative arts shows how people once lived, what they wore, their furniture, even their musical instruments and armour. Arts in every medium, from iron to silk, spotlight the outstanding craftsmanship of the Middle Ages and Renaissance. If your taste runs more to the contemporary, you'll find works of the Impressionists and post-Impressionist painters in the castle, too. Or opt for the Villa Reale (see page 64), facing Giardini Pubblici, just past the legendary Quadrilatero della Moda – itself worth browsing as a free 'museum' of contemporary art and culture. The villa, which was Napoleon's palace when he occupied Milan, has works by Gaugin, Van Gogh, Matisse, Cézanne and Picasso.

Explore ancient history, from the prehistoric through to the Roman city sitting just under Milan's foundations, at the Civico Museo Archeologico (Archaelology Museum, see page 79). The city's only remaining pieces of the Roman city walls and one of its original towers have been excavated. Exhibits are explained, so that 21st-century visitors have a picture of how ancient societies lived.

Explore one of Italy's most amazing cemeteries, Cimitero Monumentale (see page 74), an outdoor gallery of art nouveau sculpture.Not far beyond the Porta Garibaldi railway station, its oversized and dramatically striped *portici* are hard to miss. If seeing this whets your appetite for more turn-of-the-century design (called *stile Liberty* in Italy, or known also as art nouveau), continue to wander in the streets nearby, checking out the distinctively decorated buildings.

Conclude your day with some free food at one of the bars that indulges in 'happy hour' – happy indeed for customers, who can eat their fill for the price of one drink.

When it rains

A rainy day in Milan? Think shops, think (interior) sightseeing. With a minimum of outdoor exposure, you can either purchase 'til you swoon, or choose to nurture your cultural side and spend guilt-free hours admiring artworks – both without feeling as though you ought to be out ticking more sights off your list.

Head to Milan's 'main street', Galleria Vittorio Emanuele II. Built in the middle of the 19th century, this covered shopping complex was Europe's original shopping centre. The Milanese still love it, and for many visitors its soaring glass dome and decorated shop fronts are their most vivid memory of the city. Watch the passers-by spin on the mosaic bull under the central dome, each hoping for a turn of good luck. In need of a little good fortune yourself? Place your heel in the well-worn groove, and spin once on what would be the creature's tender parts, were these not made of stone.

From the elegant shops of the Galleria, make a dash across Piazza del Duomo to the cathedral itself (see page 60), a one-stop culture/history fix that could keep you out of the rain for some time, especially if you splurge on the pricey ticket to see the treasury. Just counting the finger bones of saints takes a while, let alone admiring the exquisite gold work of the reliquaries they're stowed in. Nip downstairs from the front of the church and under Piazza del Duomo to see the palaeo-Christian baptistery excavated there. Save the roof for a better day – it's too slippery up there and you won't see anything in the rain.

Take advantage of the covered arcades and stroll over to La Rinascente (see page 67), Italy's first and most important department store. It takes its role in promoting Italian products and designers very seriously (there's an entire Alessi shop inside), and it's constantly redesigning its stores to stay at the cutting edge.

Any of the prime museums and galleries here will see you through a stormy afternoon, but some of the best include the Pinacoteca di Brera (Brera Art Museum, see page 79), the Museo Poldi Pezzoli (see page 63) or the Padiglione d'Arte Contemporanea (Contemporary Art Pavilion, see page 64).

◐ You can't beat the Galleria for exercising your credit card

47

On arrival

TIME DIFFERENCE

Milan, like the rest of Italy, follows Central European Time (CET). During Daylight Savings Time (late Mar–late Oct), clocks are set ahead one hour. Italy returns to standard CET at the end of October.

ARRIVING

By air

Visitors arrive at one of Milan's three airports – **Linate** (ⓘ (02) 7485 2200 Ⓦ www.sea-aeroportimilano.it), used mostly for European flights, **Malpensa** (ⓘ (02) 7485 2200 Ⓦ www.sea-aeroportimilano.it) for intercontinental traffic, or at nearby **Bergamo** (ⓘ (035) 326 323 Ⓦ www.sacbo.it), where many budget airlines have their base.

Malpensa is 50 km (31 miles) northwest of the city and halfway between Milan and Lake Maggiore, a handy starting place for visiting the lakes. Express buses connect Malpensa with the town of Como and several points along Lake Maggiore. Malpensa is connected to the city by the Malpensa Express train (€11, journey time 45 minutes ⓘ (028) 511 4382 Ⓦ www.malpensaexpress.it ⏱ 05.00–21.00) to Cadorna Station and the Malpensa Shuttle bus (€6, journey time 50 minutes ⓘ (025) 858 1064 Ⓦ www.airpullman.com ⏱ 05.30–00.15) to Stazione Centrale. Taxis are around €70 and are slower than the train. Official yellow-and-white taxis wait outside the arrivals area, and are the best way to the nearby town of Gallarate, where trains connect to the west shore of Lake Maggiore. Linate Airport is within the city limits, 7 km (4 1/2 miles) from Stazione Centrale. A bus connects these two points every 20 minutes (€4, journey time 30 minutes ⓘ (025) 858 7237 ⏱ 06.00–23.45). Visitors may also take bus no. 73 to San Babila metro station (€1, journey time 20 minutes ⓘ 800 808 181

🕐 06.00–01.00). Taxis are around €25 and take around 15 minutes to the centre of town. Orio al Serio Airport at Bergamo is 45 km (28 miles) east of Milan. There are regular shuttle bus connections to Stazione Centrale (€7.90, journey time 60 minutes ☎ (035) 318 472 🌐 www.autostradale.it 🕐 04.00–01.00), every 30 minutes from outside the terminal building.

By rail

Milan's **Stazione Centrale** railway station, where Eurostar and other trains (general information on all Italian trains ☎ 06 44 101 🌐 www.trenitalia.it) from the rest of Europe arrive, is on the M3 (yellow) metro line, four stops from the Duomo. Trains to Lakes Como and Maggiore leave from this station, and buses from Malpensa, Linate and Bergamo airports arrive and leave from there. Taxis wait

🔺 *Milan's railway station, Stazione Centrale*

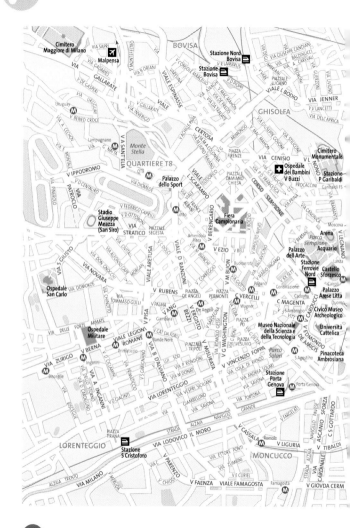

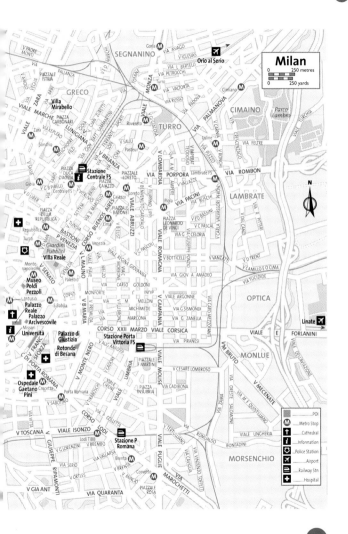

just outside the station; the minimum charge of about €3 increases at night, on holidays and for luggage. Taxis are the best way to get to your hotel after dark.

The Stazione di Cadorna, 1 km (half a mile) west of the Duomo, is on metro lines M1 and M2 (red and green respectively). As well as being the terminus of the Malpensa Express, regular trains from Como and other local towns leave from here.

By road

Long-distance buses, including Eurolines, arrive at Milan's new Lampugnano metro station (❶ (023) 008 91) on line M1 (red). Try to avoid driving in the city. Traffic is heavy and chaotic, and cars are not allowed to drive through the central area. You can drive in and out, but it is difficult to drive through the city, as it's divided into sectors. On-street parking is hard to find as many spots in the city centre are reserved for residents only (designated by yellow lines).

FINDING YOUR FEET

Milan's broad boulevards, grid layout and lack of narrow medieval streets make it relatively easy to get around. As in most major cities, avoid walking – especially alone – late at night in the areas around the railway stations or in parks or deserted areas. Most people, especially those under 40, speak a basic level of English. Many signs are posted in Italian and (often amusingly translated) English, making it easy to navigate even if you have little or no Italian.

ORIENTATION

Plan your sightseeing to begin in the heart of the city, at Piazza del Duomo, or head through the huge Galleria to Piazza della Scala. Radiating outwards, Corso Italia, (to the south), Corso Magenta

IF YOU GET LOST, TRY ...

Excuse me, do you speak English?
Mi scusi, parla inglese?
Mee skoozee, parrla eenglehzeh?

Excuse me, is this the right way to the old town/the city centre/the tourist office/the station/the bus station?
Mi scusi, questa è la strada giusta per la città vecchia/
il centro/l'ufficio informazioni turistiche/la stazione ferroviaria/
la stazione degli autobus?
*Mee skoozee, kwestah eh lah strahdah justah pehr la cheetah
vehkyah/eel chentroh/loofeecho eenfohrmahtsyonee
tooreesteekah/lah stahtsyoneh fehrohveeahreeah/
lah stahtsyoneh dehlyee owtohboos?*

(almost due west), and Via Alessandro Manzoni (heading northeast in the direction of Stazione Centrale railway station) divide the city into neat zones. These three main avenues are used as boundary lines for the three areas of the city described in this book.

GETTING AROUND
ATM operates the metro (*Metropolitana*), as well as buses and trams. Tickets can be purchased at news-stands, tobacconists, bars and at vending machines in the metro itself. A ticket is valid for 75 minutes on unlimited trams and buses, but can be used only once on the metro. If you plan to use public transport more than three times in one day, get a day ticket (*biglietto giornaliero*, €3), which is validated only on first use and can be used on any vehicle.

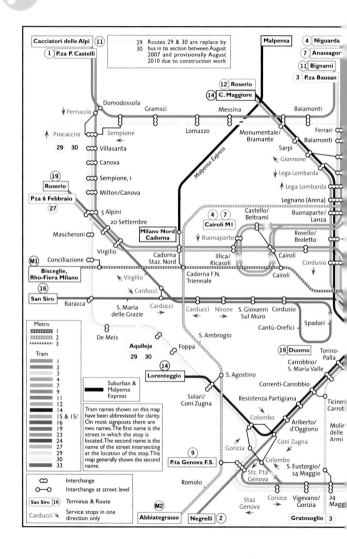

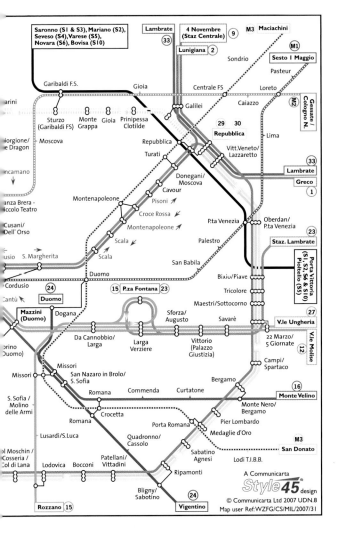

Saronno (S1 & S3), Mariano (S2),
Seveso (S4), Varese (S5),
Novara (S6), Bovisa (S10)

Lambrate 33

4 Novembre
(Staz Centrale) 9

M3 Maciachini

M1

Lunigiana 2

Sondrio

Sesto I Maggio

Pasteur

Garibaldi F.S.

Gioia

Centrale FS

Loreto

M2
Gessate /
Cologno N.

arini

Sturzo
(Garibaldi FS)

Monte
Grappa

Gioia

Prinipessa
Clotilde

Galilei

Caiazzo

iorgione/
e Dragon

Moscova

29   30
Repubblica

Lima

incamano

Repubblica

Vitt.Veneto/
Lazzaretto

33

anza Brera -
iccolo Teatro

Turati

Lambrate

Greco 1

Cusani/
Dell' Oro

Donegani/
Moscova

Cavour

Montenapoleone

Pisoni ↗

Croce Rossa ↙

Montenapoleone ↗

P.ta Venezia

Oberdan/
P.ta Venezia 23

usio   S. Margherita

Scala

Palestro

Staz. Lambrate

Scala

San Babila

Porta Vittoria
(S1, S2, S6 & S10)
Pioltello (S5)

Cordusio

Duomo

Bixio/Piave

Cantù

24

Duomo

15 P.za Fontana 23

Tricolore

V.le Ungheria 27

Mazzini
(Duomo)

Dogana

Sforza/
Augusto

Maestri/Sottocorno

orino
Duomo)

Da Cannobbio/
Larga

Larga
Verziere

Vittorio
(Palazzo
Giustizia)

Savarè

22 Marzo/
5 Giornate

Vie Molise 12

Missori

San Nazaro in Brolo/
S. Sofia

Bergamo

Campi/
Spartaco

Missori

Romana

Commenda

Curtatone

Monte Velino 16

S. Sofia /
Molino
delle Armi

Crocetta

Porta Romana

Monte Nero/
Bergamo

Romana

Pier Lombardo

Lusardi/S.Luca

Quadronno/
Cassolo

Medaglie d'Oro

M3
San Donato

ol Moschin /
Cosseria /
Col di Lana

Lodovica

Bocconi

Patellani/
Vittadini

Sabatino
Agnesi

Lodi T.I.B.B.

Ripamonti

A Communicarta
Style 45 design

Rozzano 15

Bligny/
Sabotino

24
Vigentino

© Communicarta Ltd 2007 UDN.8
Map user Ref:WZFG/CS/MIL/2007/31

A two-day ticket (*biglietto bi-giornaliero*, €5.50) is even better value.

The metro runs until about midnight, while buses and trams run about an hour longer. Use the **Radiobus**, a minivan that you can telephone to pick you up at a designated Radiobus stop, from 20.00 until 02.00 to get from the centre to anywhere else in the city (⏱ (02) 4803 4803 ⓦ www.atm-mi.it/ATM/eng/Muoversi/Radiobus ⓘ reserve up to three days in advance, €3 per person). For more information, pop into one of the three **ATM info points** (ⓢ Duomo ⓜ Metro: 1, 3; ⓢ Cadorna ⓜ Metro: 1, 2; ⓢ Centrale ⓜ Metro: 2, 3).

Most major sights can be seen from the seats of the old-fashioned hop-on-hop-off **CiaoMilano tram** (ⓢ Piazza Castello ⏱ (02) 7200 2584 🕐 11.00 & 13.00, plus Apr–Oct at 15.00). Alternatively, book a seat on Milan's City Sightseeing bus. This three-hour ride hits all the city's top sights, and includes entrance to Da Vinci's *Last Supper*. Book through the tourist office (see page 150). Tour leaves Piazza del Duomo at 09.30 and costs €50 per person.

Taxis are plentiful. Go to the nearest taxi rank (look for a black-and-white or orange sign) or telephone (⏱ (02) 4040 or (02) 8585). Use only white taxis and do not use any touted by people inside stations. All taxis here are metered.

CAR HIRE

While a car is more bother than it's worth in the city, it is the best (and in some places the only) way to explore the surrounding lakes. All major car-hire agencies are at the arrivals halls of Malpensa, Linate and Bergamo airports, including **Europcar** (⏱ 199 307 030 ⓦ www.europcar.it) and **Hertz** (⏱ 027 020 0256 ⓦ www.hertz.it).

▶ *A detail from Casa degli Omenoni*

Piazza del Duomo & East Milan

However you define the true soul of Milan – society, fashion, shopping, commerce or religion – you'll find it centred in this part of the city, between Piazza del Duomo and the enormous Stazione Centrale railway terminal, and stretching east to the suburbs.

SIGHTS & ATTRACTIONS

Major sights in eastern Milan cluster within a few minutes' walk, but do stray beyond the Duomo–Quadrilatero della Moda streets to find the city's quirkier reaches. Discover unsung churches with cool, quiet, art-filled interiors and the more worldly pleasures of boutiques, cafés, bars and design houses.

Casa del Manzoni

The doorway and exterior of author Alessandro Manzoni's home, just around the corner from Casa degli Omenoni, are elegantly decorated and worth a walk past. Manzoni's best-known work, *I Promessi Sposi (The Promised Bride)* is a must-read for Italian students. ⓐ Via Morone 1 ⓣ (02) 8646 0403 ⓛ 09.00–12.00, 14.00–18.00 Tues–Fri, closed Sat–Mon ⓜ Metro: 1, 3 to Duomo

Casa degli Omenoni

One of Milan's most startling buildings, where stone giants lean out at street level to intimidate passers-by. The house was designed by sculptor Leone Leoni in 1567. The interior is not open to the public, but the exterior is enough! ⓐ Via Degli Omenoni 3 ⓜ Metro: 1, 3 to Duomo

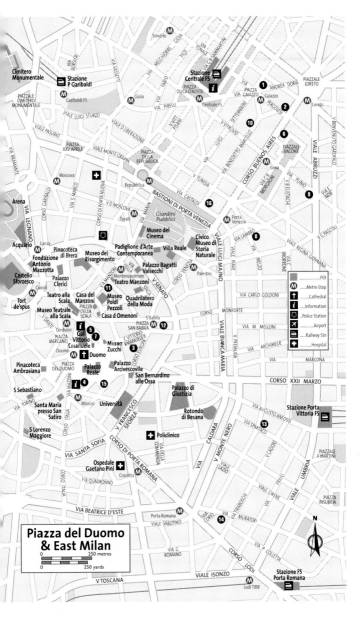

Piazza del Duomo
& East Milan

0   250 metres
0   250 yards

Duomo

The only way to take in the Duomo is to walk around its interior. On the left side, in the north transept, is one of the cathedral's greatest treasures, the *Trivulzio Candelabra*, a masterpiece of 12th-century goldsmithing.

Underneath Piazza del Duomo (accessed by a passageway inside the front of the Duomo), a palaeochristian **baptistery** (09.30–17.00. Admission charge) has been excavated. Mosaics and patterned marble floors remain and glass cases hold stone carving and other artefacts.

Outside, on the south wall, is the entrance to the stairs and lift to the **terrazzo** (09.00–17.45 Mar–Oct; 09.00–16.15 Nov–Feb. Admission charge). Up on the roof, the saint's eye panorama over Milan is spectacular. Piazza del Duomo (02) 8646 3456 07.00–18.45 Metro: 1, 3 to Duomo; tram: 1, 2, 3, 12, 24

Galleria Vittorio Emanuele II

'*Il salotto di Milano*' is what the locals call it: Milan's parlour, and there's no better place in the city to watch the world go by. Shop or browse for silk ties, furs, gold jewellery or art books in impeccably turned-out shops, and stop to look – or aim your camera – straight up into its 48-m (157-ft) dome. Piazza del Duomo 24 hrs, Shops 10.00–19.30 Mon–Sat, closed Sun Metro: 1, 3 to Duomo; tram: 1, 2, 3, 12, 24

Palazzo Reale

Facing the south side of the Duomo, beside the tourist office, this 18th-century pile was the palace of the Archduke of Austria in the late 1700s. Piazza del Duomo (02) 3932 2737 Metro: 1, 3 to Duomo; tram: 1, 2, 3, 12, 24

◆ *Vertiginous views from the Duomo's rooftop*

Quadrilatero della Moda (Fashion Quarter)

Watch out for bag-snatchers while exploring the streets south of Piazza Cavour, enclosed by Via Montenapoleone, Via della Spiga, Via Sant'Andrea and Via Manzoni to see the window displays in the great fashion houses. This district is interspersed with beautiful old *palazzi*. Ⓜ Metro: 3 to Montenapoleone; tram: 1, 2

San Bernardino alle Ossa

The main attraction of this baroque church is the bizarre chapel to the right, its walls decorated in elaborate patterns of human skulls and assorted bones. Its beginnings were pretty straightforward: the neighbouring hospital's cemetery was bursting, and they built

◉ *La Scala – the opera house*

a small room to store the exhumed bones in the church. One thing led to another, and they became the décor. ❷ Via Verziere 2 ❶ (02) 7602 3735 ❺ 07.30–13.00 Mon–Sat, 09.30–12.30 Sun ❻ Metro: 1, 3 to Duomo; tram: 12, 23, 27

Teatro alla Scala (La Scala Opera House)

Milan's cultural centrepiece has premiered the greats since its inception in 1778. Carrara marble and elaborate chandeliers gleam from 2004's thorough face wash. Absorb the fascinating La Scala museum (see page 64), or nip next door to the small church of San Giuseppe, on Via Verdi. ❷ Piazza della Scala ❶ (02) 7200 3744 ❿ www.teatroallascala.org ❺ Open for performances only ❻ Metro: 1, 3 to Duomo; tram: 1, 2

CULTURE

Fondazione Antonio Mazzotta (Antonio Mazzotta Foundation)

A rotating exhibition space for modern art, featuring everything from 20th-century Indian paintings to showings of Egon Schiele and Paul Klee. ❷ Foro Buonaparte 50 ❶ (02) 878 197 ❿ www.mazzotta.it ❺ 09.00–19.00 Wed, Fri–Sun, 10.00–22.00 Tues & Thur, closed Mon ❻ Metro: 2 to Lanza; bus: 57, 61; tram: 3, 7, 12, 14

Museo Poldi Pezzoli

Fine arts are mixed with collections of everything from Lombard enamels to armour and textiles. Free audio-tours are available in English. ❷ Via Manzoni 12 ❶ (02) 794 889 ❿ www.museopoldipezzoli.it ❺ 10.00–18.00 Tues–Sun, closed Mon ❻ Metro: 3 to Montenapoleone. Admission charge, discount on Wed

Museo Teatrale alla Scala

This famed museum next to Milan's grand theatre houses original designer sketches for costumes and stage sets. ❸ Largo Ghiringhelli 1, Piazza della Scala ❶ (02) 8879 2473 ❹ 09.00–12.30, 13.30–17.30 ❼ Metro: 1, 3 to Duomo; tram: 1, 2. Admission charge

Padiglione d'Arte Contemporanea (Contemporary Art Pavilion)

A splendid contemporary art museum featuring rotating international exhibitions and artist revivals. Art is celebrated in all its forms, from photo to video to installations. ❷ Via Palestro 14 ❶ (02) 7600 9085 ❹ 14.30–19.30 Mon, 09.30–19.30 Tues & Wed, Fri–Sun, 09.30–22.30 Thur ❼ Metro: 1 to Palestro; bus: 94; tram: 1, 2, 9, 11, 29, 30. Admission charge

Palazzo Bagatti Valsecchi

Almost a museum within a museum, this *palazzo* was the home of two 19th-century brothers who devoted much of their lives to building and furnishing it in the style of three centuries earlier. Signage, in English, describes the pieces themselves, which include tapestries, rare manuscripts, paintings by the Renaissance masters and a complete armoury. ❷ Via Santo Spirito 10 ❶ (02) 7600 6132 ❽ www.museobagattivalsecchi.org ❹ 13.00–17.45 Tues–Sun, closed Mon & Aug ❼ Metro: 3 to Montenapoleone; tram: 1. Admission charge, reduced Wed, and valid for a second day return if stamped

Villa Reale

After major restorations, Villa Reale once again glitters as it did when it was the residence of Napoleon and of the Italian kings. Amid its marble, stuccowork and crystal chandeliers is a collection of 19th- to early 20th-century art, including works by Gaugin, Van Gogh, Matisse, Cézanne and Picasso. ❸ Via Palestro 16 ❶ (02) 7600 4275 ❺ 09.00–17.30 Tues–Sun, closed Mon ❽ Metro: 1 to Palestro; bus: 94; tram: 1, 2, 9, 11, 29, 30

RETAIL THERAPY

You may require therapy (or resuscitation) after a spree in the rarified air of the world's fashion capital, the Quadrilatero della Moda.

Belfe&Belfe Not just for climbers and hikers, B&B's leisure and sportswear is as durable as it is smart. ❸ Via San Pietro all'Orto 7 (off Corso Vittorio Emanuele II) ❶ (02) 781 023 ❽ Metro: 1, 3 to Duomo

Dolce & Gabbana Famous fans include Madonna and Isabella Rossellini. Look for vintage designs at Via della Spiga 28; menswear is at Corso Venezia 15. ❸ Via della Spiga 2 ❶ (02) 7600 1155 ❽ Metro: 1 to San Babila, 3 to Montenapoleone

Emanuele A traffic-free shopping zone between Piazza del Duomo and Piazza San Babila, with small covered galleries branching off to each side. Head over to Corso Buenos Aires for more affordable wares. ❽ Metro: 1, 3 to Duomo

I Santi An outlet at the factory, where you can see the leather goods made and buy cut-price handbags, suitcases and more. ❸ Via Corio 2 ❶ (02) 5416 981 ❺ 08.30–12.30, 13.30–17.30 Mon–Fri, closed Sat & Sun ❽ Metro: 3 to Porta Romana

⬥ *Milan's Galleria was Italy's first shopping centre*

Miu Miu For funky younger fashion, head to Prada's sister line, Miu Miu. ⓐ Via Sant'Andrea 21 (off Via della Spiga) ⓣ (02) 7600 1799 ⓦ www.miumiu.com Ⓝ Metro: 1 to San Babila; bus: 73

Prada Milan's quintessential fashion name. For the latest men's and women's lines, as well as shoes, head to their flagship store in the Galleria. ⓐ Galleria Vittorio Emanuele II 63–65 ⓣ (02) 878 979 Ⓝ Metro: 1, 3 to Duomo; tram: 1, 2

La Rinascente Inside Italy's oldest department store is a collection of the latest and best of everything Italian, in a very stylish setting. Go to the top floor for the best views of the Duomo's spired rooftop. ⓐ Piazza del Duomo ⓣ (02) 88 521 ⓦ www.rinascente.it ⓛ 10.00–21.00 ⓝ Metro: 1, 3 to Duomo

Te' Con Amiche Consignments of worn-once fashions and samples of top designer wear are sold at big discounts. ⓐ Via Visconti di Modrone 33 ⓣ (02) 7733 1506 ⓝ Metro: 1 to San Babila; bus: 73

TAKING A BREAK

Art Factory Café £ ❶ Some go for the music that's provided by the city's best young DJs, but those in the know go for the grub. Think, if you will, indoor picnic. No, don't think – eat. ⓐ Via Andrea Doria 17 ⓣ (02) 669 4578 ⓛ 07.30–14.30 Mon–Sat, 18.00–22.00 Sun ⓝ Metro: 2 to Loreto

La Bottega del Gelato £ ❷ The best place to go for ice cream in Milan. Enough said. ⓐ Via Pergolesi 3 ⓣ (02) 2940 0076 ⓛ 09.00–22.00 Thur–Tues, closed Wed ⓝ Metro: 2 to Loreto

Ciao £ ❸ Cakes and sweets are the speciality of this café, not far from Piazza Fontana. ⓐ Corso Europa ⓣ (02) 12 332 6287 ⓛ 10.00–22.00 ⓝ Metro: 1, 3 to Duomo

Jungle Juice £ ❹ Just off Piazza del Duomo, this is the place to head for smoothies, freshly-squeezed juices and unusual salads. ⓐ Via Dogana 1 ⓣ (02) 8699 6809 ⓛ 10.30–19.30 Mon–Sat, closed Sun ⓝ Metro: 1, 3 to Duomo; tram: 12, 15, 24

Luini £ ❺ Stop in for a *panzerotto*, a heavenly snack of pizza dough stuffed with tomato and mozzerella. ❸ Via S Radegonda 16 (off Piazza del Duomo) ❶ (02) 8646 1917 ❿ www.luini.it ❹ 10.00–15.00 Mon, 10.00–20.00 Tues–Sat, closed Sun & Aug ❷ Metro: 1, 3 to Duomo

Spontini £ ❻ Order by the slice (*al trancio*) at Milan's favourite pizza joint. It's been here over 50 years. ❸ Corso Buenos Aires 60 ❶ (02) 204 7444 ❹ 11.45–14.15 Tues–Sun, 18.00–23.00 Tues–Fri & Sun, 19.00–00.30 Sat, closed Mon ❷ Metro: 2 to Loreto

Agnello ££ ❼ Primarily pizza, but also known for risotto; you can get a full meal or a snack in this *pizzeria* right behind the Duomo. ❸ Via Agnello 8 ❶ (02) 8646 1656 ❹ 11.00–14.00, 17.30–22.00 Wed–Mon, closed Tues ❷ Metro: 1, 3 to Duomo; bus: 50, 54; tram: 1, 2, 3

Art Deco Café ££ ❽ Even the *beau monde* have to take a break sometimes, and, when they do, they head for this self-consciously – but undeniably – cool joint. Well worth a visit for the people-watching and the delicious salads and soups. ❸ Via Lambro 7 ❶ (02) 2952 4760 ❹ 18.00–02.00 ❷ Metro: 1 to Porta Venezia

Bar Basso ££ ❾ This establishment, which becomes a suave bar in the evening (see page 71) does a nourishing line in plentiful, daytime snacks. ❸ Via Plinio 29 ❶ (02) 2940 0580 ❹ 09.00–01.00 Wed–Mon, closed Tues ❷ Metro: Lima

Frijenno Magnanno ££ ❿ Pizzas and *calzone* (folded pizzas) make up most of the menu at this relaxed venue not far from Stazione Centrale. ❸ Via Benedetto Marcello 93 ❶ (02) 2940 3654 ❹ 10.00–22.00 Tues–Sun, closed Mon ❷ Metro: 2 to Caiazzo

● *You may be forced to give in to temptation in an elegant café*

Emporio Armani Café £££ ⓫ Everything here is stylish, from the building and décor to the people who shop in this Armani complex. ⓐ Via Manzoni 31 ⓣ (02) 7231 8680 ⓛ 10.00–17.30 Mon–Sat, closed Sun Ⓜ Metro: 3 to Montenapoleone

AFTER DARK

Italy's only gay street, Via Sammartini, next to Stazione Centrale, has more than its share of nightlife, and Corso Vittorio Emanuele II has the city's densest concentration of cinemas. The Ripamonte district has a growing number of music venues.

ZUCCA IN GALLERIA

If you're the sort of person to whom the invitation 'Fancy a quick one before dinner?' raises hopes only of a nice liqueur with a few olives, you may wish to pay homage to this beautiful, art deco landmark. For it was here, in the late 19th century, that a certain Gaspare Campari debuted what he really should have trade-marked the *aperitivo* – a rhubarb-based concoction that, despite its famed aroma of cough mixture, remains temptingly moreish. ⓐ Piazza del Duomo 21 ⓣ (02) 8646 4435 ⓛ 07.00–20.00 Tues–Sun, closed Mon ⓜ Metro: 1, 3 to Duomo; tram: 1, 2, 3, 12, 24

RESTAURANTS

Brek £ ⑫ Healthy salads, grilled meat, freshly cooked mains. Unlike others in this small chain of wholesome, bright restaurants, this one has table service. ⓐ Via del Duca Cino 5 (off Via Senato) ⓣ (02) 7602 3379 ⓛ 11.30–15.00, 18.30–22.00 Mon–Sat, closed Sun ⓜ Metro: 1 to San Babila

Il Rondine £ ⑬ The huge menu and the mouth-watering, home-made recipes are to die for. A local institution. ⓐ Via Spartaco 11 ⓣ (02) 5518 4533 ⓛ 12.30–14.30, 19.30–23.00 Tues–Sat, closed Sun & Mon ⓜ Bus: 84, 169; tram: 9

Giulio Pane e Ojo £–££ ⑭ This outstanding Roman restaurant offers home-made pastas, grilled meats and a luxurious, candlelit atmosphere. ⓐ Via Muratori 10 ⓣ (02) 545 6189 ⓦ www.giuliopaneojo.com ⓛ 12.30–14.30, 20.30–00.30

(two sittings only, at 20.30 & 22.30) Mon–Sat, closed Sun ⓜ Metro: 3 to Porta Romana; tram: 9, 29, 30 ❶ reservations strongly recommended

Giardino di Giada ££ ⓯ Possibly the best Chinese food in Milan, but at a price. Located a short walk from Piazza del Duomo. ⓐ Via Palazzo Reale 5 ❶ (02) 805 3891 ⓦ www.giardinodigiada.it ⓛ 12.00–14.30, 19.30–22.30 Tues–Sun, closed Mon ⓜ Metro: 1, 3 to Duomo; bus: 54; tram: 12, 15, 27

Joia £££ ⓰ Vegans and vegetarians have a well-established, top-class Milanese restaurant that caters with imaginative dishes – and has won a Michelin star for it. ⓐ Via Castaldi 18 ❶ (02) 2952 2124 ⓦ www.joia.it ⓛ 12.00–14.30 Mon–Fri, 19.30–23.00 Mon–Sat, closed Sun, 3 weeks in Aug & 25 Dec–6 Jan ⓜ Metro: 3 to Repubblica; tram: 9, 11, 29, 30

BARS, CLUBS & DISCOS

Afterline Anyone, gay or straight, is welcome here and at most of the other gay clubs on this street. ⓐ Via Sammartini 25 ❶ (02) 669 2130 ⓛ 22.00–late ⓜ Metro: 2, 3 to Stazione Centrale

Bar Basso A bar that's been popular for more than three generations; choose the speciality, their *Negroni sbagliato* cocktail, made with *spumante* (sparkling wine) rather than traditional gin. ⓐ Via Plinio 39 ❶ (02) 2940 0580 ⓛ 20.00–01.00 Wed–Mon, closed Tues ⓦ www.barbasso.com ⓜ Metro: 2 to Lima

Dolce & Gabbana Martini Bar You might be sipping your *aperitivo* next to the latest supermodel in this ultra-swanky fashion bar. Whoever is slouched in the leather seats next to you will be *alta moda* – and well aware of it. ⓐ Corso Venezia 15 ❶ (02) 7601 1154 ⓛ 12.00–22.30 Mon–Sat, closed Sun ⓜ Metro: 1 to San Babila

Jumpin' Jazz Ballroom Live jazz for Saturday night dancing makes this worth a trip to the 'burbs. ➌ Viale Monza 140 ➊ (334) 311 2926 ➓ www.jumpinjazz.it ➐ 20.30–00.02 Sat nights only ➎ Bus: 44, 199

Magazzini Generali International acts such as Jarvis Cocker, Casino Royale and Kaiser Chiefs play here and it's popular for club nights. Friday is house music with a largely gay crowd. ➌ Via Pietrasanta 14 ➊ (02) 5521 1313 ➓ www.magazzinigenerali.it ➐ 23.30–04.00 Wed, Fri & Sat, closed Mon, Tues, Thurs & Sun, July & Aug ➎ Bus: 90, 91, 92, 93; tram: 24 ➊ Free entrance on Wednesday nights

Plastic Take care how you dress, or even the hefty admission fee won't get you into the trendiest of the trendy. Music changes according to the night and the DJ. ➌ Viale Umbria 120 ➊ (02) 733 996 ➓ www.thisisplastic.com ➐ 24.00–05.00 Thur–Sat, 20.00–02.00 Sun, closed Mon–Wed, July & Aug ➎ Bus: 90, 91, 92, 93

Ragno d'Oro Grab a cocktail and sprawl on luxurious floor cushions within Milan's old city walls. Live DJs and cool kids make for an outstanding evening. ➌ Piazzale Medaglie d'Oro 2 ➊ (02) 5405 0004 ➓ www.ragnodoro.it ➐ 18.00–02.00 ➎ Metro: 3 to Porta Romana; tram: 9, 29, 30

Rocket DJs spin rock and electro, and after shows you'll find indie artists playing here when they are in town. ➌ Via Pezzotti 52 ➊ (02) 8950 3509 ➓ www.therocket.it ➐ 23.00–03.00, closed Aug ➎ Tram: 15

La Salumeria della Musica Cabaret and live music (including jazz) bring a young crowd to this old Ripamonti factory. ➌ Via Pasinetti 2

🕿 (02) 5680 7350 🌐 www.lasalumeriadellamusica.com 🕑 21.00–01.00 Mon–Sat, closed Sun 🚌 Bus: 95; tram: 24

CINEMAS & THEATRES

Corso Vittorio Emanuele II, between the Duomo and Piazza San Babila, is Cinema Alley, with not only the most theatres but also the biggest. Wander the streets to check out what's playing where, although most films will be dubbed in Italian.

Spazio Oberdan Recently refurbished as a *Cineteca*, or film library, this classic old movie house is again showing rare vintage flicks. 🚏 Viale Vittorio Veneto 2 🕿 (02) 7740 6300 🌐 www.cinetecamilano.it 🚋 Tram: 9, 11, 29, 30

Teatro Manzoni Along with evening performances of artists singing selections from their latest albums, Teatro Manzoni offers Sunday morning *Apertivo in Concerto* jazz concerts. 🚏 Via Manzoni 42 🕿 (02) 7600 0231 🌐 www.teatromanzoni.it 🚇 Metro: 1 to San Babila or Palestro, 3 to Montenapoleone; bus: 61, 94; tram: 1, 2

Teatro alla Scala To perform at La Scala is the life goal of any opera singer. To get a ticket for a good seat is the goal of opera-lovers. To be there on opening night, 7 December, is the right of anyone who's anyone in Milan society. Along with the opera, the philharmonic orchestra, Filarmonica della Scala, performs at La Scala. Tickets for the latter run as low as €5, while opera tickets are €10–€170; the lower the price, the higher the seat, and the upper balconies are a dizzying distance and pitch above the stage. 🚏 Piazza della Scala 🕿 (02) 7200 3744 🌐 www.teatroallascala.org 🚇 Metro: 1, 3 to Duomo; bus: 61; tram: 1, 2

Castello Sforzesco & Northwest Milan

From the tight little streets of Brera to the open green spaces of Parco Sempione, the northwest neighbourhoods of Milan are filled with variety – and surprises. No one would guess, for example, that Brera's close-packed buildings hide a lush botanic garden (see page 78). This is a part of the city worth exploring on foot, since its main sights are all within walking distance of each other.

SIGHTS & ATTRACTIONS

Castello Sforzesco

The Sforza Castle is actually a fortified palace inside a walled enclosure. From within its walls the Visconti and the Sforza families ruled much of northern Italy from the Middle Ages until 1500. Inside are frescoes in the *loggia* of the Corte Ducale (Dukes' Court) and a display of ornamental stone carving. The Tort de' spus, or Wedding Cake Fountain, stands in front of Castello Sforzesco and is one of the prettiest in Italy. The castle museums (🕓 09.30–17.30 Tues–Sun, closed Mon. Admission charge) include a museum of ancient art together with the Egyptian and Prehistoric sections of Milan's Archaeological Museum. 🔢 Piazza Castello 📞 (02) 8846 3703 🕓 Castle grounds: 07.00–19.00 Ⓜ Metro: 1, 2 to Cadorna, 1 to Cairoli; bus: 43, 57, 58; tram: 1, 3, 4

Cimitero Monumentale

The tombs here are amazing. The entrance is impressive, and many of the monuments that mark the final resting places of the once rich and famous are in the art nouveau style. A map, in English,

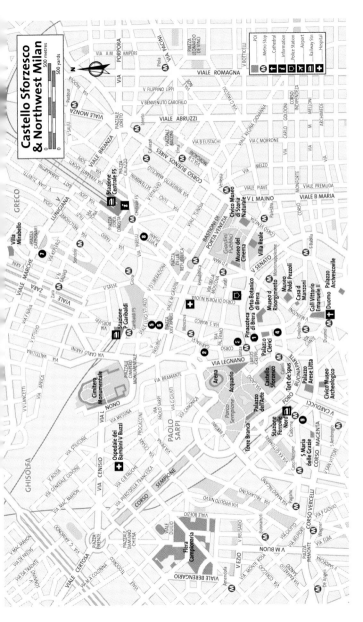

⬤ *You don't see many cemeteries as stylish as Cimitero Monumentale*

leads to some of the best, many by noted Italian sculptors.
ⓐ Piazzale Cimitero Monumentale (north of Stazione Porta Garibaldi)
ⓣ (02) 659 9938 ⓞ 08.30–17.15 Tues–Fri, 08.30–17.45 Sat & Sun,
closed Mon ⓥ Tram: 3, 4

Palazzo dell'Arte (Triennale)

The building, constructed to house the premier Italian design show
every third year, works well as a showcase for art and design. Inside
there are always high-level shows and exhibitions, often international
in scope. ⓐ Viale Alemagna 6 (in Parco Sempione) ⓣ (02) 7243 4208
ⓦ www.triennale.it (tickets at ⓦ www.biglietteria@triennale.it)

🕐 Hours vary according to current show Ⓜ Metro: 1, 2 to Cadorna. Admission charge

Parco Sempione

Along with the Triennale, the leafy expanses of this rare patch of green in central Milan can't quite hide the strange Torre Branca (see page 78). If you like art nouveau, be sure to see the fanciful aquarium pavilion at the Via Gadio edge of the park. Free Wi-Fi, paid for by the city, now covers the entire park area. ⓐ Between Castello & Corso Sempione 🕐 07.00–sunset Ⓜ Metro: 1, 2 to Cadorna, 1 to Cairoli; tram: 1, 3, 4

Santa Maria delle Grazie

Although nearly everyone comes here to see one of the world's most famous paintings, *The Last Supper*, in the adjoining monastery, the church itself is not without interest. The architect Bramante gave the 15th-century Gothic church a makeover, with a new façade, a rebuilt sanctuary and the delightful little 'Frog Cloister' behind the church. Inside, in the second chapel on the right, a Caravaggio painting (a treasure in its own right) stands in for the Titian stolen by Napoleon's army in 1797 and taken off to the Louvre, from which it has never been returned.

You'll need to reserve well in advance to look inside the Cenacolo Vinciano, which houses Leonardo da Vinci's *The Last Supper*, but do make the effort as it's considered one of the great masterpieces of Western art. ⓐ Piazza Santa Maria delle Grazie ⓘ (02) 8942 1146 🕐 Church 08.00–19.30, Cenacolo 09.00–18.00 Mon–Fri, 09.00–14.00 Sat, closed Sun Ⓜ Metro: 1 to Conciliazione; tram: 24 ❶ Timed Cenacolo tickets must be reserved in advance; operators speak English. Admission charge

Torre Branca

Designed by famed architect Gio Ponte and his associates, the tower was built to celebrate the 1933 Triennale art exhibition. Closed since the early 1970s, a rush of money from Milanese distillers, Fratelli Branca, completely restored it. The view of Milan and the Alps, if the day is clear, is worth the €3. ❷ Viale Camoens ❶ (02) 331 4120 Ⓦ www.branca.it/torre ❸ 10.30–12.30, 16.00–18.30 Wed, 10.30–13.00, 15.00–18.30 & 20.30–24.00 Sat, 10.30–14.00, 14.30–19.00 Sun, mid-Oct–mid-Apr; 10.30–12.30, 16.00–18.30 & 21.30–01.00 Wed, 14.30–18.30, 21.30–01.00 Fri, 10.30–14.00, 14.30–19.30 & 21.30–01.00 Sun, mid-Apr–mid-Oct; 21.30–01.00 Tues & Thur, mid-May–mid-Oct Ⓜ Metro: 1, 2 to Cadorna; tram: 1, 3, 4 ❶ closed during bad weather. Admission charge

ORTO BOTANICO DI BRERA

An astonishing variety of plant species, including Europe's oldest ginkgo tree, are hidden in the inner courtyard of the huge Brera museum and art school; and yet from the outside you wouldn't even know it was there. Forming a quiet, green oasis, the gardens also house the Merz telescope through which astronomer Giovanni Virginio Schiaparelli elaborated his theory of life on Mars. Thus you have the possibility of alienating whoever is lucky enough to be travelling with you by declaring, 'Ah! *Hortus Botannicus Braidensis*, if I'm not very much mistaken' and reviving that much-admired David Bowie impression. ❸ Via Brera 28 ❶ (02) 8901 0419 Ⓦ www.horti.unimore.it ❸ 09.00–12.00, 13.00–16.00 Mon–Fri, closed Sat & Sun Ⓜ Metro: 2 to Lanza, 3 to Montenapoleone

CULTURE

Civiche Raccolte d'Arte Antica del Castello (Art Museum)

The exhibitions in the many different art museums inside the castle vary from medieval stone to wooden carvings, and all are pretty remarkable. Most outstanding – and enough reason for a visit – is Michelangelo's enormously moving *Rondanini Pietà*. The artist was working on it just a few days before his death. ⓐ Castello Sforzesco, Piazza Castello ⓣ (02) 861 125 ⓛ 09.00–17.30 Tues–Sun, closed Mon ⓜ Metro: 1, 2 to Cadorna, 1 to Cairoli. Admission charge

Civico Museo Archeologico (Archaelology Museum)

The highlights of the museum are its Roman works, including a 24-sided Roman tower, Torre Ansperto. There's a lot more of the ancient world in the museum, which also includes the church of San Maurizio itself, where you can see the excellent frescoes by Bernardo Luini and his sons that almost completely cover the interior in vivid colours. ⓐ Corso Magenta 15 ⓣ (02) 8645 0011 ⓛ Museum 09.00–13.00, 14.00–17.30 Tues–Sun, closed Mon, Church 09.00–12.00, 14.00–17.30 Tues–Sun, closed Mon ⓜ Metro: 1, 2 to Cadorna. Admission charge to the museum

Pinacoteca di Brera (Brera Art Museum)

All the great Italian painters – Titian, Raphael, Caravaggio, Tintoretto, Veronese, Luini, Tiepolo, Canaletto – are represented in the massive collection here, the largest in the city. ⓐ Via Brera 28 ⓣ (02) 722 631 ⓦ www.brera.beniculturali.it ⓛ 08.30–19.15 Tues–Sun, closed Mon; may vary according to exhibition ⓜ Metro: 2 to Lanza, 1 to Montenapoleone. Admission charge

⬤ Cool off by the Wedding Cake Fountain

RETAIL THERAPY

The narrow streets near Pinacoteca di Brera are peppered with many a tasty antique shop. Beyond Parco Sempione, Corso Vercelli has some neat boutiques; check Via Belfiore, off Corso Vercelli, for shoes. Via Canonica, in the Paolo Sarpi area, Milan's former Chinatown, is littered with leather shops and crafts studios.

10 Corso Como Outlet Not the ultra-pricey main store, but a cut-price outlet on the street between Stazione Porta Garibaldi and Cimiterio Monumentale. The same high-quality styles for men and women, but last season's lines. ⓐ Via Tazzoli 3 ⓣ (02) 2900 2674 ⓛ Fri–Sun pm (hours vary), closed Mon–Thur & Fri–Sun am ⓜ Metro: 2 to Garibaldi; bus: 41; tram: 3, 4, 11

Cappelleria Melegari Head to this amazing bonce-boutique for hats to suit every occasion and every cranium. And if hats aren't your bag, there are also ties, belts and gloves. ⓐ Via Paolo Sarpi 19 ⓣ (02) 312 094 ⓦ www.cappelleriamelegari.com ⓛ 10.00–19.00 Tues–Sun, closed Mon ⓜ Metro: 2 to Moscova

Cargo & High Tech One of the most fun stores in Milan: candles, clothes, furniture, soaps and more are sprawled over lots of little rooms. ⓐ Piazza XXV Aprile 12 ⓣ (02) 624 1101 ⓦ www.cargomilano.it ⓛ 10.30–19.30 Tues–Sun, closed Mon ⓜ Metro: 2 to Garibaldi

Il Cucchiaio di Legno The 'Wooden Spoon' sells everything a fanatical foodie may need: balsamic vinegar, olive wood bowls, truffles, teas and more. ⓐ Via Ponte Vetero 13 (off Foro Buonaparte)

ℹ (02) 8738 8670 🌐 www.ilcucchiaiodilegno.it 🕐 10.00–19.00
Tues–Sat, closed Sun & Mon 🚍 Bus: 61; tram: 1, 3, 12, 14, 17

Dcube Stocking an array of designer objects, Dcube is the place
to pick up unusual gifts, such as silicone coffee cups or flower-
shaped baking pans. 🏠 Via Ponte Vetero 17 ℹ (02) 8909 6297
🌐 www.dcubedesign.it 🕐 12.30–19.30 Sun & Mon, 10.00–19.30
Tues–Sat 🚍 Bus: 61; tram: 1, 3, 12, 14, 17

La Piccola Legatoria Beautifully bound notebooks and paper-covered
boxes in lively colours and smart designs make easy-to-carry-home
gifts. 🏠 Via Palermo 11 ℹ (02) 861 113 🌐 www.lapiccolalegatoria.it
🕐 10.00–19.00 Tues–Sat, closed Sun & Mon 🚇 Metro: 2 to Lanza

TAKING A BREAK

Cafés and little bars that do a nice sandwich are plentiful, especially
in the shopping streets of Brera and around Corso Vercelli. They are
less glitzy than those closer to Piazza del Duomo, but still offer
a good mix of styles.

Bar Jamaica £ ❶ A favourite with the liberal literary crowd of the
1960s, this Brera bar has a charm that has endured the passage
of time. 🏠 Via Brera 32 ℹ (02) 876 723 🕐 08.00–02.00 Mon–Sat,
08.00–20.30 Sun 🚍 Bus: 61

Moscatelli £ ❷ An outstanding wine bar with loads of old-school
charisma. Go for a glass of wine at happy hour and enjoy their
home-made Milanese snacks. 🏠 Corso Garibaldi 93 ℹ (02) 655 2602
🕐 10.00–02.00 Mon–Sat, closed Sun 🚇 Metro: 2 to Moscova; bus: 43, 94

Castello Sforzesco

⬥ *There are many intimate restaurants tucked away in the side streets*

Viel £ ❸ For incredible ice cream, smooth sorbet and fresh fruit juices, head to Viel. Perfect during Milan's sweltering summer heat.
ⓐ Corso Garibaldi 12 ❶ (02) 8691 5489 ⓦ www.viel-milano.com
🕓 08.00–01.00 Tues, Thur–Sun, 08.00–19.30 Mon, closed Wed
Ⓝ Metro: 2 to Lanza; bus: 43, 94

Da Claudio ££ ❹ The best *pescheria* (fresh fish store) in the city, da Claudio serves up an all-day *aperitivo* of exquisite snack plates.
ⓐ Via Ponte Vetero 16 ❶ (02) 8056 857 ⓦ www.pescheriadaclaudio.it
🕓 11.00–22.00 Ⓝ Bus: 61; tram: 1, 3, 12, 14, 17

Corso Como Café ££–£££ ❺ Stop in at the Corso Como complex, at least to have coffee or a cocktail in Carla Sozzani's courtyard café. Be sure you're well dressed – you never know who you'll be sitting next to!
ⓐ Corso Como 10 ❶ (02) 653 531 🕓 08.00–22.00 Ⓝ Metro: 2 to Garibaldi

AFTER DARK

Some of the hottest nightclubs are in the streets near the Castello, and restaurants hide on the small streets off the major avenues.

RESTAURANTS

Pizzeria di Porta Garibaldi £ ❻ Hand-made *gnocchi* (potato dumplings) and crusty pizza, available by the slice, make this a good choice for day or evening. ⓐ Corso Como 6 ❶ (02) 655 1926
🕓 12.00–14.30, 19.00–01.00 Tues–Sun, closed Mon & one week in Aug Ⓝ Metro: 2 to Garibaldi

Casa Fontana ££ ❼ Risotto Milanese is the city's signature dish, and you won't find it in more varieties anywhere else: here it's offered in more than 20 permutations. Piazza Carbonari 5 (02) 670 4710 www.23risotti.it 12.00–14.30 Tues–Fri & Sun, 19.30–22.30 Tues–Sun, closed Mon Metro: 3 to Sondrio; bus: 727

Tomoyoshi Endo ££ Head here for some of the best Japanese food in the city. The sushi is fantastic, but be sure to peruse their full menu in the evening for delicacies such as tuna cheek baked in a salt crust. Via Vittor Pisani 13 (02) 6698 6117 www.tomoyoshi-endo.com 12.00–15.00, 19.00–23.00 Mon–Sat, closed Sun Metro: 3 to Repubblica or Centrale

Osteria La Carbonella da Santo £££ Known for their outstanding grilled meats and risotto with white truffles, sourced from nearby Alba. Via Terraggio 9 (02) 861 835 12.15–14.30 Mon–Fri, 19.15–24.00 Mon–Sat, closed Sun Metro: 1, 2 to Cadorna; bus: 50, 58, 94

BARS, CLUBS & DISCOS

Alcatraz Big-name groups, usually Italian and European, play during the week; at weekends it's DJs with dance music. Via Valtellina 25 (02) 6901 6352 www.alcatrazmilano.com 22.00–late Wed, Fri & Sat, closed Sun–Tues & Thur Metro: 3 to Maciachini; bus: 41, 46, 51, 52, 70, 82, 90, 91, 92; tram: 3, 4, 11

Blue Note This intimate jazz club draws a full house for live performances by well-known soloists and groups. Via Borsieri 37 (just south of Piazza Segrino) (02) 6901 6888 www.bluenotemilano.com Live shows 21.00 & 23.30 Mon–Sat, 21.00 Sun Metro: 3 to Zara

Hollywood A dance club that has managed to stay *au courant* since the 1980s, despite the tiny premises and whopping entrance fee. Tuesday is R'n'B night. Corso Como 15 (02) 6598 996 www.discotecahollywood.com 22.00–late Metro: 2 to Garibaldi

Roialto A stylish crowd of 30-somethings packs the bar after work for the Caribbean-style drinks and bountiful free buffet. Via Piero della Francesca 55 (02) 3493 6616 www.mastmilano.it 18.00–02.00 Tues–Sat, 12.00–22.00 Sun, closed Mon Tram: 11; bus: 43, 57, 169

THEATRES

Piccolo Teatro/Teatro Strehler European theatre groups perform dramatic works at this Brera venue, in an exciting and interesting year-round schedule. Largo Greppi (02) 7233 3222 www.piccoloteatro.org Metro: 2 to Lanza

Teatro Smeraldo A venue for popular music and dance performances, Teatro Smeraldo hosts top international touring shows and solo acts. Piazza XXV Aprile 10 (02) 2900 6767 www.smeraldo.it Metro: 2 to Garibaldi

Teatro Dal Verme Classical concerts are performed by touring groups and a variety of local music companies, from quartets to the symphony, in a small theatre near Castello Sforzesco. Via San Giovanni sul Muro 2 (02) 87 905 www.dalverme.org Metro: 1 to Cairoli

Southwest Milan & the Navigli

Don't let the number of churches in this part of Milan scare you.
They contain some of the most interesting sights in the city,
including a fantastic trick played by the greatest of Milan's
Renaissance architects, Bramante. Making up for all the art and
culture south of the Duomo is the seriously swinging Navigli
neighbourhood alongside the old canal. The nightlife is fun and
affordable, with a varied mix of venues to suit all ages and tastes.
Closer to the Duomo, spend some time in the tangle of small streets
between it and the university to experience a more characterful
Milan – and to discover restaurants and cafés filled with locals.
The old docks area, the Ticinese, is now a mix of boutiques, studios,
trendy cafés and smart restaurants.

The two museums in southwestern Milan offer, between them,
something for everybody.

SIGHTS & ATTRACTIONS

The Navigli

Thank Leonardo da Vinci for one of the city's liveliest settings for
after-hours fun, especially in good weather. He designed some of
the canals that helped make Milan the economic power it still is,
by giving it access to water transport. The barges are gone, but
you can still ride on a boat through the canals from Alzaia Naviglio
Grande to see part of the old maritime quarter. The three lines
which navigate through 50 km (31 miles) of the canal system run
from May through to September. ⓐ Alzaia Naviglio Grande 4
ⓣ (02) 6679 131 ⓦ www.naviglilombardi.it ⓝ Tram: 9, 29, 30

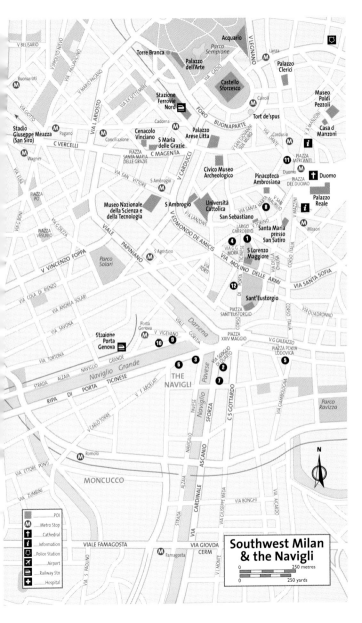

Piazza Mercanti

Hardly anything medieval in Milan is left, thanks to wars and zealous renewal projects, making this little enclave opposite the 16th-century law courts even more charming. On one side is the 1233 Palazzo della Ragione, political centre of medieval Milan; the black-and-white marble Palazzo degli Osii, built in 1316, forms the other side. The colonnaded open area was the market.
ⓐ Just off Piazza del Duomo Ⓝ Metro: 1, 3 to Duomo

Sant'Ambrogio

After the Duomo, this is considered to be Milan's most significant church. Highlights are the intricate carvings on the tops of the portico columns, the carved 4th-century Stilicone sarcophagus under the pulpit and the gold altarpiece by master goldsmiths in the time of Charlemagne. Through the last chapel on the right is the vivid mosaic dome of the original 4th-century Sacello de San Vittore.
ⓐ Piazza Sant'Ambrogio 15 ⓘ (02) 8645 0895 ⓛ 07.00–12.00, 14.00–19.00 Mon–Sat, 07.00–13.15, 14.30–19.45 Sun Ⓝ Metro: 2 to Sant'Ambrogio. Admission charge for Sacello de San Vittore

Sant'Eustorgio

In one of the repeated foreign raids on Milan, Sant'Eustorgio was sacked, and the relics of the Magi, which it had been built to house, were carted off. But this story takes an unexpected twist, because they were much later returned, and are still the centre of a festival on Epiphany (6 Jan). Balduccio's marble tomb of Stefano Visconti is an outstanding example of high Gothic, but the masterpiece that brings art lovers to the church is the Cappella Portinari, Milan's first

▶ *The Navigli of Milan*

real Renaissance room. ⓐ Piazza Sant'Eustorgio 1 ❶ (02) 5810 1583 ⓦ www.santeustorgio.it ❷ Church 07.45–12.00, 15.30–18.30, Chapel 10.00–18.00 Tues–Sun, Sept–June, closed Mon; 16.00–18.30 July–Aug ⓜ Tram: 3. Admission charge for chapel

San Lorenzo Maggiore

San Lorenzo is an example of early Christian basilica design, even though it has been changed over the centuries. The chapel of Sant'Aquilino, to the right near the entrance, still shows the original 4th-century mosaic decorations. In front of the basilica are Milan's best Roman remains, 2nd-century columns, part of a temple or a public bath that were moved here in the 4th century. ⓐ Corso di Porta Ticinese ❶ (02) 8940 4129 ❷ 07.30–12.30, 14.30–18.45 Mon–Sat, 07.30–18.45 Sun ⓜ Metro: 2 to Sant'Ambrogio; tram: 3, 20. Admission charge

Santa Maria presso San Satiro

It's hard to get any sense of the personalities of great historical figures and artists, but after seeing this church, it's easy to believe that Bramante had a sense of humour: step inside and your eye can't help but be drawn to the majestic, deep, vaulted sanctuary that stretches into an apse almost as long as the main part of the church itself. Keep your eye on it as you walk forward, and watch it melt into an almost flat wall. Even when you know in advance that it's all a stucco illusion, it looks so real that you doubt what you've seen. ⓐ Via Torino 9 ❶ (02) 7202 1804 ❷ 08.30–11.30, 15.30–17.30 Mon–Sat, 09.30–10.30, 16.30–17.30 Sun ⓜ Metro: 1, 3 to Duomo

Stadio Giuseppe Meazza (San Siro Stadium)

Football fans can see inside the stadium on guided tours and brush up on the history of both Milan's famed teams (Inter and AC Milan)

● *Sant'Ambrogio*

at the Hall Of Fame. With a ticket to the match, the museum is free until 30 minutes before kick-off. ⓐ Via Piccolomini 5 ❶ (02) 404 2432 ⓦ www.sansirotour.com ⏱ 10.00–17.00 (may vary on match days) Ⓜ Metro: 1 to Lotto; tram: 24. Admission charge

CULTURE

Museo Nazionale della Scienza e della Tecnologia Leonardo da Vinci (National Museum of Science and Technology)

You don't have to be a techie to love this museum, with its 10,000-strong selection of exhibits. The highlights are the works of Leonardo da Vinci. Thirty different models and reconstructions show his impact on later – even modern – technology. ⓐ Via San Vittore 21 ⓘ (02) 485 551 ⓦ www.museoscienza.org ⓛ 09.30–17.00 Tues–Fri, 09.30–18.30 Sat & Sun, closed Mon ⓜ Metro: 2 to Sant'Ambrogio; bus: 50, 54, 58, 94. Admission charge

Pinacoteca Ambrosiana (Ambrosiana Art Museum)

Based on the private collections of a cardinal, who built this museum in the early 1600s, the galleries are split between a priceless collection of early manuscripts and the paintings and drawings. Paintings by da Vinci, Botticelli and Tiziano are among the highlights. ⓐ Piazza Pio XI 2 ⓘ (02) 806 921 ⓛ 10.00–17.30 Tues–Sat, closed Sun & Mon ⓜ Metro: 1, 3 to Duomo; tram: 12, 24. Admission charge

RETAIL THERAPY

Stretching southwest from the Duomo, Via Torino is one of the city's main shopping streets, especially for shoes. Shops are aimed at a youngish set, and include all price ranges. At the far end of Via Torino is the Ticinese area, filled with artisans' studios and small speciality shops. From Largo Carrobbio, Corso di Porta Ticinese leads to the Navigli, another area with artisans' workshops.

Antiques and collectables are the focus of the street market, the last Sunday of each month along the Naviglio Grande canal.

Serious collectors go to the antique shops behind Sant'Ambrogio along Via Santa Marta and Via Lanzone. On Via San Giovanni sul Muro you'll find smaller items, in shops that often specialise in one type of antique, such as glassware or scientific instruments.

Papier Pop around the corner from Via Torino to pick up hand-made paper, picture frames, bags and more. ➋ Via San Maurilio 4 ➊ (02) 865 221 ⏰ 15.00–19.00 Mon, 10.00–13.00, 15.00–19.00 Tues–Sat, closed Sun ⏷ Tram: 2, 3, 14

Papiniano Market The popular street market has everything from food and homewares to cut-price designer labels. ➋ Viale Papiniano ⏰ 08.30–13.00 Tues & Sat ⏷ Metro: 2 to Sant'Agostino; tram: 20, 29, 30

OH BEJ! OH BEJ!

This fabulous market and street party, which sets up every December in Piazza Sant'Ambrogio, is held in celebration of the city's patron saint, Ambrose. Now, Ambrose is said to have had a way with words and was known as a sweet-talking guy, which is, apparently, why so many sugary sweets are on sale here (parents, take note). But there's a wide range of other edible delicacies, as well as clothes and many a potential Christmas present to be snapped up. In Milan, the festive season kicks off here, and there's an atmosphere of bonhomie that you don't find in the Christmas sales back home. The name, if you're wondering, comes from the Milanese pronounciation of the Italian for 'Ooh, lovely!'

Purple Vintage clothing and a wide range of top styles from Italian designers. Don't miss the weird and wonderful window displays, which often include unusual toys. ➌ Corso di Porta Ticinese 22 ☎ (02) 8942 4476 Ⓦ www.purpleshop.it 🕐 15.30–19.00 Mon–Sat, 10.30–12.30 Tues–Sat, closed Sun

TAKING A BREAK

The canal banks are lined with cafés and *pizzerias*, so there's no shortage of places to stop for a few nibbles. Some bars have abundant (free) food in the early evening, while others may serve up simply a bowl of crisps or a few olives.

20 (Vente) £ ❶ Trendy, arty (part bar, part gallery) and welcoming, 20 offers enough food to go with *aperitivi* that it may well replace dinner altogether. Wednesday sees drinks and buffet for €5, and occasional cult films. ➌ Via Celestino IV 9 (at Via Gian Giacomo Mora, off Corso di Porta Ticinese) ☎ (02) 837 6591 🕐 18.00–24.00 🚋 Tram: 2, 3, 14

La Briocheria di Rajmondo £ ❷ Ask for *brioche* (Milanese for croissant), filled (*sfoglitelle di ricotta*) or plain, or grab a slice of pizza for a pick-up. You'll have to eat it on the canal embankment, since there are no tables. ➌ Via Scoglio di Quarto 3 ☎ (338) 406 5217 🕐 Until 02.00 🚋 Tram: 9, 29, 30

Rinomata Gelateria £ ❸ A beautiful, old *gelateria* that has crowds spilling out the door most of the year. ➌ Ripa di Porta Ticinese, corner of Viale Gorizia ☎ (02) 5811 3877 🕐 11.00–23.00 🚋 Tram: 9, 29, 30

◗ *Catching the sun in Piazza Mercanti*

Cuore ££ ❹ Fabulous snacks, cocktails and two floors of unusual artworks make this a hidden gem. ⓐ Via Gian Giacomo Mora 3 ⓘ (02) 5810 5126 ⓦ www.cuore.it ⓛ 18.00–02.00 ⓝ Tram: 2, 3, 14

Gattullo ££ ❺ A long-time favourite for really good *panettone*, plus other pastries, salads and *aperitivi*. ⓐ Piazza Porta Lodovica 2 ⓘ (02) 5831 0497 ⓦ www.gattullo.it ⓛ 07.00–22.00 Tues–Sun, closed Mon ⓝ Bus: 79, 169; tram: 9, 15

Pizzeria Tradizionale ££ ❻ The name pretty much sums it up, although they do serve a few fish dishes. ⓐ Ripa di Porta Ticinese 7 ⓘ (02) 839 5133 ⓛ 11.00–23.00 ⓝ Metro: 2 to Porta Genova

El Tropico Latino ££ ❼ With tables alongside the canal, this Mexican bar is a popular stop for cocktails and nachos. ⓐ Via Ascanio Sforza 31 ⓘ (02) 5810 4000 ⓛ 12.00–24.00 ⓝ Bus: 59, 71, 169, 325; tram: 9

AFTER DARK

The old canal area, the Navigli, thrives in the hours after sunset (although you'll find its cafés open in the daytime, too). Music overflows into the streets, as do the throngs of 20- and 30-somethings that keep the area so lively.

RESTAURANTS

Although there are plenty of flashy high-end restaurants in these neighbourhoods, especially around the Navigli, you'll also find cosy *trattorias* catering to the locals. Look for these as you sightsee during the day, in the cross streets between the Duomo and Sant'Ambrogio, as well as in the tiny alleys around the canals.

Govinda £ ❽ Vegetarian dishes are served in this no-alcohol restaurant operated by the Hare Krishna organisation. Go for the outstanding value lunch, which includes four different dishes, juice, home-made bread and tea. ❷ Via Valpetrosa 3 (just off Via Torino) ❶ (02) 862 417 ❼ www.harekrsna.it ❻ 12.30–14.30, 19.30–22.00 Tues–Sat, closed Sun & Mon ❽ Tram: 2, 3, 14

Pizzeria Premiata £ ❾ Head down the sloping drive to this fabulous *pizzeria*, a favourite with locals. ❷ Via Alzaia Naviglio Grande 2 ❶ (02) 8940 0648 ❻ 12.30–14.30, 19.30–23.00 Wed–Mon, closed Tues ❽ Metro: 2 to Porta Genova; tram: 9, 29, 30

Al Coniglio Bianco ££ ❿ A cosy little *trattoria* just off one of the main canals, with a groovy canal-side terrace. ❷ Alzaia Naviglio Grande 12 ❶ (02) 5810 0910 ❻ 19.30–22.30 Wed–Mon, 12.30–14.30 Sat & Sun, closed Tues ❽ Metro: 2 to Porta Genova; tram: 9, 29, 30

Al Mercante ££ ⓫ Warm, cosy interior, with tables on the medieval Piazza Mercanti in good weather. Local specialities are delicious and carefully prepared. ❷ Piazza Mercanti 17 ❶ (02) 805 2198 ❼ www.ristorantealmercante.it ❻ 12.00–14.30, 19.00–22.30 Mon–Sat, closed Sun ❽ Metro: 1, 3 to Duomo

Trattoria Toscana ££ ⓬ Head through the narrow entrance and empty front room to an attractive open-air, candlelit dining room where Tuscan and traditional dishes from northern Italy are well prepared. Outstanding ambience. ❷ Corso di Porta Ticinese 58 ❶ (02) 8940 6292 ❼ www.trattoriatoscana.net ❻ Restaurant & bar 19.00–01.00 Mon–Sat, Bar only 19.00–02.00 Sun ❽ Bus: 94; tram: 3

BARS, CLUBS & DISCOS

Le Biciclette Modern art mixes with contemporary and experimental music aimed at the young professional and arty set that come here for the lingering happy hour (18.00–22.00) and stay for the show. ⓐ Via Torti at Conca del Naviglio ⓣ (02) 839 4177 ⓛ 18.30–24.00 Mon–Sat, 12.30–15.00 Sun brunch ⓝ Bus: 94; tram: 2, 14

Divina The décor is over the top and the music is mixed by well-known DJs, making this one of the best nightspots for dancing till dawn. ⓐ Via Molino delle Armi, corner of Via della Chiusa ⓣ (02) 5843 1823 ⓦ www.divina.biz ⓛ 23.30–04.00 Thur–Sat, closed Sun–Wed ⓝ Bus: 94; tram: 15

Scimmie Beside the canal in Navigli, with nightly live blues, rock and jazz, this is one of the city's best-known clubs. ⓐ Via Ascanio Sforza 49 ⓣ (02) 8940 2874 ⓦ www.scimmie.it ⓛ 18.30–late Mon–Sat, closed Sun ⓝ Metro: 2 to Porta Genova

Le Trottoir A hopping, late-night joint with live music, crazy art installations and eccentric atmosphere. ⓐ Piazza XXIV Maggio 1 ⓣ (02) 837 8166 ⓦ www.letrottoir.it ⓛ 11.00–02.00 ⓝ Tram: 9, 15, 29, 30

▶ *A Roman bridge over a gorge, Lake Como*

Lake Como

Romans fled sultry Mediolanum (Milan) in the summer for Lake Como's cooling breezes, and it remains a popular idea today. The Roman villas have been replaced by more modern ones, some built by royalty, some now owned by film stars and some that you can stay in. Perhaps the prettiest of Italy's lakes, Como is shaped like an upside down letter Y, deep and narrow and tightly enclosed between tall mountains. Views are simply spectacular from nearly anywhere – except the northern part of the lake, where the shore flattens out. Even in winter, the climate is mild and the shores are still green. In the spring and summer, flowers bloom everywhere, especially in the microclimate of the Tremezzina Riviera, and many of the villa gardens are open to view.

GETTING THERE

By rail
Como is close enough that travellers can stay in town and visit Milan on day trips should they wish. Trains run every 30 minutes from Milan's Stazione Centrale to Como's Stazione San Giovanni, a ten-minute walk from the lake shore; the ride takes about 40 minutes. Additional trains ply the route from Milan's Stazione Nord to Como's more centrally located Stazione Lago Nord, near the ferry dock, and are timed to meet the ferries.

By road
Most driving visitors arrive in the pretty working town of Como, 50 km (31 miles) via the A9 north of Milan (a 45-minute journey). Local buses and roads spread from here around the lake to

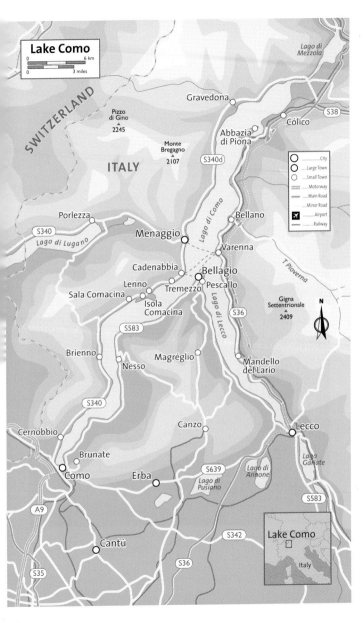

● *View of Lake Como from Brunate*

Bellagio, Tremezzo and beyond. Como's southeast arm is less interesting, but you can bypass it with a car ferry to Varenna. **Rullo Bike** (ⓔ Via Grandi ⓣ (031) 263 025) hires out two-wheelers.

By water

Frequent ferries (ⓔ Navigazione Lago di Como, Via Cernobbio ⓣ (031) 579 211 ⓦ www.navigazionelaghi.it) visit most of the lakeside towns, and a day's excursion gives time enough to look around several, since most attractions are within walking distance of the ferry landing. Economical day passes allow multiple stops. Detailed timetables are available from the tourist information office at Piazza Cavour (see page 150).

COMO

Trains from Milan arrive in Como, and although it's tempting to hop aboard a waiting boat to explore the lake, Como is worth a little time. The Cortesella, its old commercial streets that radiate from the shore, are still filled with interesting shops. At its centre is the **Duomo** (ⓔ Piazza del Duomo ⓣ (031) 265 244 ⓛ 08.00–12.00, 15.00–19.00), perhaps the best example anywhere of how 14th-century Gothic styles slipped into the Renaissance. At the centre of the leafy and walkable lakeshore promenade is Piazza Cavour, filled with cafés. Right on the shore, the temple-shaped building is Tempio Voltiano, a memorial/museum to native son Alessandro Volta (as in electric volt). In front of it is a moving and sombre Holocaust Memorial, with quotes from victims in several languages, and a reminder of the many Italians among them. The promenade park continues to Villa Olmo, with its extensive and colourful gardens that are also a public park.

ENJOYING COMO ON FOOT

Walking paths for all levels of energy are everywhere – short walking routes along the shore, high hikes along the mountainsides above. Some lead to sights missed by road-bound travellers, including huge boulders dropped by glaciers, castle ruins, waterfalls, Roman roads and Iron Age rock engravings. Several good walks begin in Bellagio, from a 20-minute amble to the tiny fishing village of **Pescallo**, the oldest settlement on that peninsula with waterside cafés and *trattorie*, to a strenuous hour rewarded by views of all three branches of the lake from the **Mulini del Perlo**. Walking guides are available from the local tourist offices, including those at Como and Bellagio.

CULTURE

Como's pleasures are more active and scenic than they are cultural, although some fine works of art hide in churches, and the occasional villa is open to view. But two good museums in Como are worth a stop for those interested in their subjects: silk and early history.

Museo Archeologico e Storica (Archaeological and Historic Museum)

Two *palazzi* are chock-full of artefacts and exhibits, one giving a fascinating look at the early inhabitants of the lakes in Neolithic times, with tools and implements excavated nearby. Roman relics complete the picture of early Como, at the time of Julius Caesar.
ⓐ Piazza Medalgie d'Oro ⓣ (031) 271 343 ⓛ 09.30–12.30, 14.00–17.00 Tues–Sat, 10.00–13.00 Sun, closed Mon. Admission charge

Museo Didattico della Seta (Silk Museum)

Silk has been an important part of Como's economy since the 1500s, and the story of its manufacture fills this surprisingly interesting museum. Displays take visitors through the method of printing with the patterns that make Como silk distinctive.
ⓐ Via Diaz 84 ⓣ (031) 269 869 ⓦ www.museosetacomo.com
ⓛ 09.00–12.00, 15.00–18.00 Tues–Fri, closed Sat–Mon
ⓝ Bus: 7. Admission charge

RETAIL THERAPY

The best thing to buy in Como is silk; the only question is where to buy it. Browse the shops in the old Cortesella to get an idea of what you like, then hit the markets. Silk goods to look for include women's scarves, dresses and blouses, lingerie and men's shirts and ties.

Frey Silk clothing, scarves and accessories are in the factory store of a renowned Como firm, well located in the Old Town.
ⓐ Via Garibaldi 10 ⓣ (031) 267 012 ⓦ www.frey.it ⓛ 10.00–12.30, 14.30–19.00 Mon–Sat, closed Sun

Idearte Porcelain and fine ceramics. The onsite kiln means that you can personalise pottery to take home. ⓐ Piazza Roma 35
ⓣ (031) 426 951 ⓛ 10.00–18.00 Mon–Sat, closed Sun

Mantero Fine silks from the firm that supplies the big fashion names, including Nina Ricci. ⓐ Via San Abbondio ⓣ (031) 32 11
ⓦ www.mantero.com ⓛ 10.00–12.30, 14.30–19.00 Mon–Sat, closed Sun

Markets On Tuesday and Thursday mornings and all day Saturday, the pavements along the old city walls of Viale Battisti and Viale Cattaneo become a street market, where you can find everything from clothing to hairbrushes. Be careful of pickpockets here. On Saturdays (except the first one each month) local craftspeople gather to sell in Piazza San Fedele, in central Como. The last Saturday of each month fills the streets and *piazze* with antiques vendors, creating gargantuan traffic jams. Don't plan to drive to your hotel then.

TAKING A BREAK

Como, like every lake shore town, has a clutch of cafés lining the pavement and on terraces over the water. Along with coffee and stronger stuff, most of these serve snacks and sandwiches.

L'Altro Café £ Panini and *piadini* sandwiches and internet access in a relaxed and friendly setting. ❸ Via Diaz 28 ❶ (031) 260 664 ❺ 12.00–20.00

Caffè Nova Comum £ Cosy café for coffee or *gelato* during the day, until the stylish business crowds arrive for *aperitivi*. ❷ Piazza del Duomo 2 ❶ (031) 260 483 ❺ 08.00–22.00

La Goccia £ Casual café and restaurant with streetside tables. Inexpensive lunch menus and hearty soups. ❷ Via Rusconi 18 ❶ (031) 261 800 ❺ 10.00–19.00 Mon–Sat, closed Sun

Lostrano Bar £ Nice place to stop for a drink, with live music occasionally late in the evening. ❸ Via Adamo del Pero 8 ❶ (031) 249 429 ❺ 08.00–22.00 Tues–Sat, closed Sun & Mon

⬥ *Enjoy a relaxed meal overlooking Lake Como*

Novecento Cafè £ *Aperitivi* and a wide selection of teas, unusual in Italy. Foods include panini sandwiches and crêpes. ⓐ Viale Lecco 23 ⓘ (031) 266 228 ⓛ 11.00–22.00 Tues–Sun, closed Mon

Pub Greenwich £ A casual, central pub, where you can stop for a drink, a light meal or a ponder about how on earth they came up with the name. ⓐ Piazza Giuseppe Terragni ⓘ (031) 267 872 ⓛ 11.00–23.00

Il Solito Posto ££ Local favourites, including an *osso bucco* that's positively oozing marrow and hand-made seasonal ravioli. ⓐ Via Lambertenghi ⓘ (031) 271 352 ⓛ 12.00–15.30, 19.00–22.00 Wed–Mon, closed Tues

AFTER DARK

Como offers some good places to hear music, and its restaurants are good. Don't expect the glamour of more urban nightspots, but don't expect the prices, either. And the fashion police don't guard the doors.

Restaurants

Osteria del Gallo £–££ Sample outstanding local wines by the glass at the bar or at a table, accompanied by a plate of individually prepared tapas. ⊜ Via Vittani 16 ⊕ (031) 272 591 ⊕ 18.00–22.00

Ristorante Hosterietta ££ Risotto is the house speciality, available in a wide selection of combinations, including one with roasted red chicory. ⊜ Piazza Volta 57 ⊕ (031) 241 516 ⊕ 12.30–14.30, 19.30–22.30 Mon–Sat, closed Sun

Bars, clubs & discos

Il Birrificio di Como A cavernous microbrewery where you can see beer being made and sample the latest recipes. It has an equally capacious beer garden. ⊜ Via Paoli 3 ⊕ (031) 505 050 ⊛ www.ilbirrificio.it ⊕ 12.00–14.30, 19.00–01.00 Sun–Thur, 19.00–02.00 Fri & Sat

Cactus Juice Tex-mex diner and party house with famed cocktails. Terrace eating in summer and late-night dancing most weekends. ⊜ Via Mentana 2 ⊕ (031) 269 178 ⊛ www.cactusjuicecafe.com ⊕ 19.00–late

Cinemas & theatres

Como has one theatre, **Teatro Sociale** (⊜ Via Bellini ⊕ (031) 270 170 ⊛ www.teatrosocialecomo.it), although **Villa Olmo** hosts a number of concerts, performances and rehearsals. It's worth attending one just to see the interior, an impressive hall, three storeys tall with balconies. The four cinemas in Como show mostly Italian films and international blockbusters; English speakers should look for movie listings with VO (meaning 'original version') next to them.

ACCOMMODATION

Terminus ££ With all of the *belle époque* elegance of the Liberty style of architecture, this lakefront hotel in the heart of Como has pretty gardens, an elegant restaurant and an unsurpassed location.
ⓐ Lungo Lario Trieste 14 ⓣ (031) 329 111 ⓕ (031) 302 550
ⓦ www.hotelterminus-como.it

BELLAGIO

Caught in the tip of the peninsula that divides the two southern arms of the lake, Bellagio has the most perfect setting on Lake Como and it makes the best of it with picturesque streets and elegant gardens. But the somewhat self-conscious prettiness doesn't diminish the appeal of its terraced and stair-stepped narrow streets, and icing-coloured buildings filled with boutiques and cafés. Passenger and car ferries connect to both shores.

SIGHTS & ATTRACTIONS

The **Basilica di San Giacamo** is worth seeing for the detailed, 12th-century stone carving behind the altar (ⓐ Piazza della Duomo ⓣ 08.00–12.00, 15.00–19.00). A lane behind the basilica leads to the gardens of **Villa Serbelloni**, covering the hillside with formal landscaping and exotic trees that frame views across Lake Como to the Alps (ⓣ (031) 950 204 ⓘ Tours 11.00 & 15.30 by reservation, Tues–Sun, Apr–Oct, booked at the tourist information office on

Piazza della Chiesa. Admission charge). Below, along the lake, are the gardens of **Villa Melzi d'Eril**, lovely for strolling. Azaleas and rhododendrons fill it with blooms in the spring and dark cypresses hide a serene Japanese garden (ⓐ Via Melzi d'Eril 8 ⓣ (02) 8699 8647 ⓛ 09.00–18.00 Apr–Oct, closed Nov–Mar. Admission charge).

RETAIL THERAPY

Bellagio has smart shops and boutiques, but remember that this is a resort town, accustomed to moneyed clientele on holiday, so while styles may be chic, prices will be the highest on the lake.

TAKING A BREAK

Bar Café Rossi £ Smart lakeside café with superb sandwiches all day. The pastries and coffee are great for a pre-sightseeing breakfast. ⓐ Piazza Mazzini 22 ⓣ (031) 950 196 ⓛ 08.00–21.00

Bistro del Ritorno £ Pizza, sandwiches, pasta and light dishes in a relaxed, friendly place with a terrace. ⓐ Via E Vitali 8 (off Via Roma from Piazza Mazzini) ⓣ (031) 951 915 ⓛ 09.00–21.00 Tues–Sun, closed Mon

Grotta ££ Pizza, pasta and tasty main dishes in a friendly atmosphere, just off lakefront Piazza Mazzini. ⓐ Salita Gernaia ⓣ (031) 951 152 ⓛ 10.00–22.00 Tues–Sun, Jan–Oct, closed Mon & Nov & Dec

AFTER DARK

Ristorante Silvio ££ Fresh trout and other fish from the lake are the specialities at this legendary inn, a short way south of town beyond the Villa Melzi gardens. ⓐ Via Carcano 12, Localita Loppia ⓣ (031) 950 322 ⓦ www.bellagiosilvio.com

○ *Shopping in the 'high' streets of Bellagio*

ACCOMMODATION

Hotel Florence ££ A joyously friendly (yet traditionally styled) hotel in the very centre of Bellagio. Choose *aperitivi* on the gravelled lake view terrace or a soak in the jacuzzi or Turkish bath. ❸ Piazza Mazzini 46 ❶ (031) 950 342 ❶ (031) 951 722 Ⓦ www.hotelflorencebellagio.it

Grand Hotel Villa Serbelloni £££ This former villa is the essence of genteel hospitality, with exceptional service, glorious décor and its own orchestra for dancing every evening. ❸ Via Roma 1 ❶ (031) 950 216 Ⓦ www.villaserbelloni.it

🔻 *Relax in the hotel pool at Villa Serbelloni*

AROUND LAKE COMO

The lake is surrounded by charming towns and villages, and even has its own island.

BRUNATE

Creaky vintage cars of Funicolare Brunate climb at a dizzying steep pitch for more than 1,000 m (3,300 ft) from Como's lakefront to spectacular views from café terraces in the village above. Or climb the stone-paved path from the upper station to the tower at the top to see the Alps and the lakeshore towns to the north. ⓐ Funicolare Brunate, Piazza de Gasperi 4 ⓣ (031) 303 608 ⓛ 06.00–22.30. Admission charge

CERNOBBIO

On Como's western shore, Cernobbio's lakefront is dominated by villas set in gardens. The exiled English Queen Caroline stayed at the most glorious of them, Villa d'Este. Now an ultra-posh hotel, it is surrounded by elaborate Italian gardens open only to the villa's well-heeled guests. But Parco Villa Erba's gardens are open to the public at weekends. ⓐ Largo Luchino Visconti 4 ⓣ (02) 4997 7134 ⓛ 14.00–18.00 Sat, 10.00–18.00 Sun, closed Mon–Fri

ISOLA COMACINA

Mystery enshrouds the lake's only island, but through the mists of its often violent past flit a cast of characters straight out of history books: Atilla the Hun, Frederick Barbarossa, Lombard King Berringer, Queen Theodolinda, King Albert of Belgium and saints Abonde, Agrippa and Domenica. The latter three attest to its importance as a religious centre – barbarian hordes razed no fewer than five churches on the tiny island, at least one of them a Roman temple later consecrated by Christians.

The ruins there today are the remains of the churches founded by the three saints, destroyed in the 1100s. These are connected by a single trail that loops around the island, leading uphill to the highest point, and to the foundations of **Santa Maria col Portico** before dropping to the remaining churches: walls and stone floors of the medieval **Basilica di Sant'Eufemia** below the later **Oratorio di Santi Giovanni, Pietro e Paulo**. Behind it, the **palaeo-Christian baptistery** has mosaics from the time of Charlemagne. Take a picnic lunch to this moody island and wander with ghosts from the Middle Ages. There are several ferries per day from the seaside town of **Sala Comacina** (❶ (338) 459 9492 ◷ 09.00–24.00 Mar–Oct, closed Nov–Feb), where there is parking, or take a regular lake boat here (❸ Navigazione Lago di Como ❶ (031) 579 211 ◍ www.navigazionelaghi.it).

THE TREMEZZINA RIVIERA

Even milder than the rest of the lake is this stretch of western shore, where it's not unusual to see outdoor cafés filled in February. The steep hillsides behind Cadenabbia and Tremezzo are wrapped in year-round greenery and lush plants native to southern climes thrive. Centrally located and with boat service to any part of the lake, the Tremezzina Riviera makes a good base for exploring by car or boat. **Villa Carlotta** (❸ Via Regina 2, Tremezzo ❶ (034) 440 405 ◍ www.villacarlotta.it ◷ 09.00–18.00 Apr–Sept; 09.00–17.00 Mar & Oct, closed Nov–Feb. Admission charge), the 18th-century palace of Prussian Princess Carlotta, has one of northern Italy's most famous gardens. Lined by camellias, rhododendrons, palms and exotic trees, its paths open unexpectedly to show lake and mountain views, especially glorious in the early spring when everything is in full bloom.

On a point south of Tremezzo, **Villa Balbianello** (🄰 Via Regina 28
🄸 (034) 456 110 🄻 10.30–12.30, 15.30–18.30 Tues, Thur & Fri,
10.00–18.00 Sat & Sun, Apr–Oct, closed Mon & Wed & Nov–Mar.
Admission charge) sits in luxuriant, perfectly groomed grounds.
The baroque villa itself is not open to the public, but the charming
gardens are. So romantic are they, George Lucas set the love scenes
in *Star Wars, Attack of the Clones*, in the grounds. Boats leave from
nearby Lenno, or you can walk from the Lenno boat landing.

VARENNA

Car ferries shuttle across the lake into the little harbour where
Varenna's pastel buildings cluster under cliffs, connected to the
lake by a garden. The convent of **Villa Monastero** (🄸 (034) 129 5450
🄦 www.villamonastero.it 🄻 09.00–19.00 Apr–Oct, closed Nov–Mar)
abandoned since the 1500s, is planted in terraced formal gardens.

High above Varenna, 11th-century **Castello di Vezio** (🄰 Via Esino
Lario 🄸 (034) 1814 011 🄦 www.castellodivezio.it 🄻 10.00–sunset
Apr–Oct; 10.00-17.00 Sat & Sun, Nov & Mar; closed Dec–Feb.
Admission charge

TAKING A BREAK

Albergo Ristorante Il Vapore £ A family inn, serving homey, hearty
local dishes, including perfectly cooked lake fish. 🄰 Piazza T Grossi 3,
Menaggio 🄸 (034) 432 229 🄻 12.00–15.00, 18.00–20.00

Trattoria del Rana £–££ A casual, friendly *trattoria* where you'll meet
more locals than tourists over generous plates of homestyle food.
🄰 Via Monte Grappa 27, Tremezzo 🄸 (034) 440 602 🄻 12.00–14.30,
19.00–22.30 Wed–Mon, Nov–Sept, closed Tues & Oct

Gatto Nero £££ A traditional Italian meal with a view, both outstanding. A favourite with local and international celebrities. ⓐ Via Monte Santo 69, Cernobbio ⓣ (031) 512 042 ⓛ 12.30–14.30, 19.30–23.00

Lido di Lenno £££ On Friday and Saturday nights, this cool restaurant turns into a nightclub, but with no entrance charge and reasonably priced drinks. Dance on the covered dancefloor or on the beach in summer. ⓐ Via Comoedia 1, Lenno ⓣ (034) 457 093 ⓦ www.lidodilenno.com ⓛ Bar 16.00–04.00

Tartaruga £££ Near nightly events, frequent live bands and dancing until 03.00 in the morning. ⓐ Via Belvedere 12, Villa Guardia (about 20 km (12 miles) west of Como) ⓣ (031) 483 290 ⓦ www.tartaruga.com ⓛ 19.00–03.00 Thur–Sun, closed Mon–Wed

ACCOMMODATION

Hotel Regina £–££ Modern with slick, friendly service. A very family-orientated hotel with heaps of sporting activities and a private beach. Landlubbers can soak up the enchanting views from the sun terrace or the well-tended gardens. ⓐ Via Regina Levante 10, Gravedona ⓣ (034) 489 446 ⓕ (034) 490 098 ⓦ www.reginahotels.it

Villa d'Este £££ An award-winning lakeshore mansion steeped in history. The facilities are stupendous, ranging from a modern spa to an 18-hole golf course. Lakeshore private villas are also available to rent. ⓐ Via Regina 40, 22012 Cernobbio ⓣ (031) 3481 ⓕ (031) 348 844 ⓦ www.villadeste.it

---

ⓞ *Sadly, the gardens at Villa d'Este are open only to guests*

Lake Maggiore

Although Italy can't claim all of this sprawling and scenic lake, it has all but the northern tip, which lies in Switzerland. The mountains that surround it on all sides give almost every lake view a stunning backdrop. For views down on the lake and into the layers of Alps that extend beyond it, you can take cable cars from the lakeside to several of the peaks.

GETTING THERE

By rail

A variety of Swiss intercity trains (to Basle) and local Italian trains (to Domodossola on the Swiss border) leave hourly from Milan's Stazione Centrale. The journey takes around an hour. For Laveno on the eastern shore of the lake a train leaves hourly from Milan's small Cadorna station. The journey time is 90 minutes.

By road

The picturesque hub of Stresa on the more popular western side of Lake Maggiore is around 90 km (56 miles) northwest of Milan. It's about an hour's journey by car, taking the A8 towards Malpensa airport, then the A26 towards Novara and Stresa. Roads and local buses connect all the towns on the lake's shore.

By water

A variety of boat transport – steamers, hydrofoils (*corse rapide*) and car ferries (*traghetti*) – connect the shore towns (🄰 Navigazione Lago Maggiore 🄣 800 551 801 🄦 www.navigazionelaghi.it). The most popular services are the twice-hourly car ferry from Laveno to

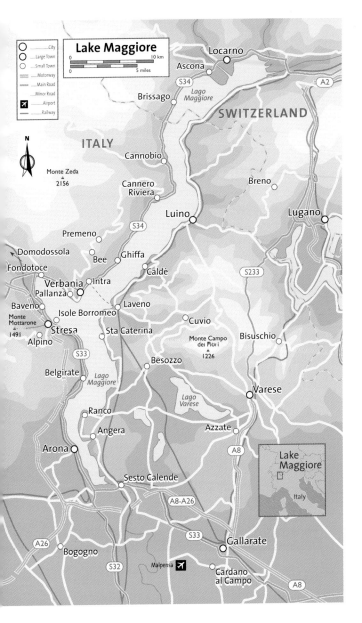

Intra/Verbania on the west shore (🕑 05.00–24.00), and the short hops to the Borromean Islands from Verbania, Stresa, Arona and Baveno (🕑 07.30–18.45). For mountain bike rental and excursions, call in at **Sapori d'Italia** (🏠 35 Via del Martini 📞 (0323) 934 642).

STRESA

Old money built Stresa, but evidently there's enough new money to keep the sumptuous digs thriving, because they fairly sparkle with fresh paint and polish. The moneyed mood is kept up in the boutiques that line its well-kept streets.

Boats leave from its waterfront for Isole Borromeo, and from Piazzale Lido, north of the centre of town, a cable car to the top of **Monte Mottarone** (🏠 Funivia il Mottarone 📞 (0323) 302 95 🌐 www.stresa-mottarone.it 🕑 09.30–17.30. Admission charge) provides beautiful views down at the hotels and the islands. From the top you can see Lakes Maggiore and Orta, plus the Alps. Stop half-way for a short walk to **Giardino Alpinia** (**Alpine Garden** 📞 (0323) 302 95 🌐 www.giardinoalpinia.it 🕑 09.30–18.00 Apr–mid-Oct, closed mid-Oct–Mar), where 800 varieties of alpine plants from

mountains all over the world cover a hilltop. Views from the gardens are good, too, and your cable car ticket includes admission.

SIGHTS & ATTRACTIONS
Parco della Villa Pallavicino
On the shore south of Stresa, sitting in a 20-ha (50-acre) park filled with more than 40 species of exotic animals and birds – kangaroos, zebras, llamas, flamingoes – and formal gardens in beds of solid colour, is this stunning villa. Children will like the petting section with baby animals. **ⓐ** Rte S33 **ⓣ** (0323) 315 33 **ⓦ** www.parcozoopallavicino.it **ⓛ** 09.00–18.00 Mar–Oct, closed Nov–Feb. Admission charge

CULTURE
Settimane Musicali di Stresa e del Lago Maggiore
(Stresa-Lake Maggiore Music Weeks)
A high-quality music festival that begins in late July and lasts to mid-September. Most of the two-dozen performances are scheduled for late August to mid-September, and they take place at Stresa, on

◯ View of Lake Maggiore from above Stresa

the two larger Borromean Islands and in other lakeside towns. For a complete schedule, contact the organisers at Ⓐ Via Carducci 38, 28838 Stresa Ⓣ (0323) 310 95 or (0323) 304 59 Ⓦ settimanemusicali.net.

RETAIL THERAPY

Stresa's streets are filled with swish little boutiques. These can be a little expensive, but, of course, it costs nothing to have a good browse.

Acqua di Stresa Selling the 'perfume of Lake Maggiore', this tiny shop is a great spot to pick up local soaps, scrubs and scents. Ⓐ Piazza Cadorna 25 Ⓣ (0323) 933 999 Ⓦ www.acqua-di-stresa.com Ⓛ 10.00–12.30, 14.30–19.30 Mon–Sat, closed Sun

Dubois Local craftsman Maurizio Colombo creates beautiful wooden toys and room decorations for children. Ⓐ Via Bolongaro 8 Ⓣ (0323) 32 099 Ⓛ 15.30–19.30 Mon, 10.00–12.30, 15.30–19.30 Tues–Sat, closed Sun

TAKING A BREAK

Finding cafés, pizza shops and snack bars is easy in any of the lake towns. Just head for the water and you're sure to find at least one occupying a terrace or perched on the shore.

El Gato Negro £ Tucked away on one of Stresa's back streets, this little café is a great place for a coffee or a glass of wine. Ⓐ Via Principessa Margherita 52 Ⓣ (0323) 33 621 Ⓛ 08.00–19.00 Mon–Sat, closed Sun

---

◀ *The cable car on Monte Mottarone overlooks Isola Bella*

AFTER DARK

Taverna del Pappagallo £–££ The pizza and *focaccia* are baked
in the wood-fired oven of this attractive family-run restaurant.
ⓐ Via Principessa Margherita 46, Stresa ❶ (0323) 304 11
Ⓦ www.tavernapappagallo.com ● 12.30–14.30, 19.30–22.30
Mon–Sat, closed Sun

Ristorante Piemontese ££–£££ In downtown Stresa, the
Piemontese has a fine collection of local speciality dishes.
Dine in their elegant dining room or on the pergola terrace.
ⓐ Via Mazzini 25 ❶ (0323) 30 235 Ⓦ www.ristorantepiemontese.com
● 19.30–22.30 Mon–Sat, closed Sun

ACCOMMODATION

Albergo Sempione £ The Albergo Sempione is on the lakefront
promenade near the pier for the Borromean Islands. Simple but
attractive, it is a good option as 12 of its 17 rooms have views of
the lake. ⓐ Corso Italia 46, Stresa ❶ (0323) 304 63 ❶ (0323) 304 63
Ⓦ www.albergosempione.it

Hotel La Luna Nel Porto ££ A wonderfully pretty villa on the lake
shore. Guests can choose between 12 individually designed suites,
some with panoramic terraces and private gardens. A bargain
for the price. ⓐ Corso Italia 60 ❶ (0323) 934 466
Ⓦ www.lalunanelporto.it

Grand Hotel des Iles Borromees £££ Built in 1861, made famous
by Hemingway's *Farewell to Arms* in 1929 and renovated in 1991,
this is the Grand Dame of the lake. Elegant and luxurious.
ⓐ Lungolago Umberto ❶ (0323) 938 938 Ⓦ www.borromees.it

⬤ *Stay in style and luxury at Grand Hotel des Iles Borromees*

ISOLA BELLA – IF IT'S CAMP YOU'RE AFTER...

Everything on this tiny island is over-the-top, from the astonishing giant Mannerist figures in the gold-and-stucco Throne Room of **Palazzo Borromeo** to the obsessively fussy outdoor terrace gardens that are tended by squadrons of master gardeners (ⓣ (0323) 305 56 ⓦ www.borromeoturismo.it ⓛ 09.00–17.30 Apr–Sept, 09.00–17.00 Oct, closed Nov–Mar. Admission charge). The *palazzo* dominates the view, and looks like the lair of a disfigured psychopath, whose only consolation is pounding his organ until an ingénue floats up the sewer. From the faux grotto – yes, that's faux grotto – on the ground floor, step out the back door into the gardens. Real nature may come as a shock after all that. When you've adjusted, climb to the top for smashing views of the palace, the lake and the patterned flowerbeds below.

VERBANIA

The former towns of Pallanza, Intra, Suna, Fondotoce, Trobaso and Possaccio make up Verbania, which sometimes makes it confusing for strangers who look for these places on a map.

SIGHTS & ATTRACTIONS

Madonna di Campagna, on the road between the Intra and Pallanza settlements, is a beautiful Romanesque church whose building spans from the 12th century to the 16th. At Fondotoce is the **Riserva Naturale di Fondotoce**, a reed-filled bird habitat at the delta of the River Toce. Footpaths and bike trails wander

through the wetlands, and tent pitches are inside the reserve.
Book for guided walks and motorboat cruises with park naturalists
at the Nature Reserve's Verbania office (ⓐ Via Canale 48, Verbania
(Fondotoce) ⓣ (0322) 496 596 ⓛ 10.00–12.00 Mon, Wed & Fri,
17.15–18.15 Tues & Thur, closed Sat & Sun). The gardens of **Villa
Táranto** (ⓐ Pallanza ⓣ (0323) 556 667 ⓦ www.villataranto.it
ⓛ 08.30–18.30 Apr–Oct, closed Nov–Mar. Admission charge)
combine the formal terraces, pools and rose gardens of Italian
gardens with the flowing lines of an English garden park filled
with thousands of exotic and native trees. The lake's mild climate
allows more than 20,000 plant varieties to grow here.

AFTER DARK

Boccon di Vino £–££ A little Slow Food *osteria* with a blackboard
menu, but a chef who knows his stuff. Whatever the day's pasta
combo is, order it. ⓐ Via Troubetzkoy 86, Verbania ⓣ (0323) 504 039
ⓛ 12.00–14.30, 19.30–22.00 Mon–Sat, closed Sun

La Latteria £–££ Moderately priced, outstanding local delights.
Grab a table in the sunshine if the weather is warm enough.
ⓐ Piazza San Rocco 20, Verbania ⓣ (0323) 53 447 ⓛ 12.30–14.30 Mon
& Tues, Thur–Sat, 19.30–22.30 Mon–Sat, closed Sun

Chi Ghinn ££ Dine while appreciating the amazing views from
Chi Ghinn's spacious terrace, or stop in for a glass of one of their
many wines. ⓐ Via Maggiore 21/23, Bee (Verbania) ⓣ (0323) 56 326
ⓦ www.chighinn.com ⓛ 12.30–14.30, 19.30–23.00 Wed–Mon,
closed Tues, Apr–Sept; 12.30–14.30, 19.30–23.00 Thur–Mon,
closed Tues & Wed, Oct–Dec & Mar, closed Jan & Feb

Piccolo Lago ££ Inspired combinations such as ravioli filled with artichoke and prawns make this modest restaurant popular.
ⓐ Via Filippo Turati 87, Fondotoce (Verbania) ❶ (0323) 586 792
ⓦ www.piccololago.it ❶ 19.00–23.30 Mon–Sat, closed Sun

ACCOMMODATION

Hotel Ancora ££ A pretty lake-view hotel by Verbania's Lungolago with superb out of season deals. Bathrooms belie the aged charm of the hotel's façade and are funky and spotless. The rooms with a view are quieter than those on the back. ⓐ Corso Mameli 65, Verbania ❶ (0323) 53 951 ⓦ www.hotelancora.it

AROUND LAKE MAGGIORE

Exploration of the areas around the lake will reveal many delightful towns, not to mention a sprinkling of intriguing little islands.

SIGHTS & ATTRACTIONS
Angera

The Borromeo family history is the history of the lake and of nearly all its towns, and you will bump into Borromeos at every turn. Meet them first in the imposing castle from which they guarded the southern entrance to the lake. The original medieval defensive structure of Rocca Borromeo (Borromeo Castle) as well as the towering Torre Castellana, are still intact. The **Museo della Bambola** (doll and children's clothes museum) is worth a look, if only for the amusing collection of turn-of-the-century French and German robots. ⓐ Via alla Rocca
❶ (0331) 931 300 ⓦ www.roccaborromeo.it ❶ 09.00–18.00 Apr–Sept; 09.00–17.30 Oct, closed Nov–Mar. Admission charge

🔺 *The entertaining Transport Museum at Ranco*

In the wonderfully quirky **Museo dei Transporti** in neighbouring Ranco, you can climb onto vintage tram cars, follow a coal-cart into a mine and admire carriages and conveyances of the formerly famous. ⓐ Off S629, Ranco ❶ (335) 8441 341 Ⓦ www.museo-ogliari.it ❶ 10.00–12.00, 14.00–18.00 Tues–Sun, closed Mon

Arona

A good base if you arrive from Milan by train, Arona has plenty of hotels and restaurants, plus good access to transport around the lake. Stop at the **Turismo** for boat schedules, maps and advice (ⓔ Piazzale Duca d'Aosta ❶ (0322) 243 601). While in town, take advantage of what may be your only opportunity to see the world through the eyes of a saint. On a hillside just north of town stands the 23.5-m-tall (77 ft) statue of **San Carlo Borromeo**. Climb the 145 stairs to the head, from which you can view the world through one eye. ⓐ Off S33, north of town ❶ 09.15–12.30, 14.00–18.30 Apr–Sept; Sat & Sun only Oct & Mar, closed Nov–Feb

Ascona

The pretty harbour with its *Lungolago* promenade is backed by an old town filled with high-end boutiques. The town claims to be one of Switzerland's sunniest spots, little wonder then that writers and artists such as Herman Hesse and Alexej Jawlensky made it their home.

Brissago

The palm-studded town barely has room to perch in the narrow space between mountain and lake, but has made room for a promenade, the *Lungolago*. More warm-climate plants grow outdoors on the nearby island, **Isole Brissago**, which lake waters keep above freezing temperatures all winter. The botanical garden houses medicinal plants, some extinct in the wild. ❶ (41) 91 791 4361 Ⓦ www.isolebrissago.ch ◷ 09.00–18.00 Mar–Oct, closed Nov–Feb ❶ go by boat from Porto Ronco, 2 km (1 mile) north of Brissago. Admission charge

Isola Madre

Let your spirit run free in the spacious and serene garden park covering most of Isola Madre. Paths lined by exotic trees wander circuitously past lawns highlighted by flowerbeds, and continue around the shore. The southern shore is a terraced promenade. The villa there is smaller and less opulent, worth touring to see the wonderful marionette theatre collections on the top floor. ❶ (0323) 312 61 Ⓦ www.borromeoturismo.it ◷ 09.00–17.30 Apr–Sept; 09.00–17.00 Oct, closed Nov–Mar. Admission charge

Isola dei Pescatori

The tiniest of the islands has no palaces and no gardens, yet the cluster of candy-coloured houses and the narrow streets will seem

⬥ *The rock promontory and shoreline at Caldè*

like paradise to most visitors. Fishing boats are tied along the shore next to several restaurants specialising in grilled lake fish. Ernest Hemingway, who wrote *A Farewell to Arms* in a nearby mainland hotel, loved this little island.

Isole Borromeo (Borromean Islands)

The undeniable highlight of the lake is this group of islands in Golfo Borromeo, near Stresa. You can see them all in one day (€11.50 for a pass to the three islands, €8.50 for any two) or make separate trips by ferry or water taxi; you can even stay overnight on the smallest (and most charming) of them, the Isola dei Pescatori. The *biglietteria* (kiosk) next to Stresa's steamer landing has tickets and details.

Laveno

A car ferry shortens driving distances around the lake by shuttling cars across to the Intra wharf in Verbania (❷ Navigazione Lago Maggiore ❶ 800 551 801 ❿ www.navigazionelaghi.it). A little bucket-like gondola carries passengers to the top of **Sasso del Ferro** for views of the lakes and mountains. One of the lake's prettiest spots is south of Laveno, the 13th-century hermitage **L'Eremo di Santa Caterina del Sasso Ballaro**, built into the face of a cliff between the villages of Cerro and Reno. Take the steep stone steps down the banking to see it, or photograph it from the lake steamer as it passes close (❶ 08.30–12.00, 14.00–18.00). To the north of Laveno, the picture-perfect little harbour of **Caldè** hides behind a rock promontory.

From Laveno, it's an easy 12 km- (7 mile-) drive to pretty little **Lago di Varese** (Lake Varese), with its reedy lake shore, birdlife and nature reserve. The old town of Azzate makes a good stop, with several cafés and fine dining.

On the way is **Villa della Porta Besozzo** (ⓐ Casalzuigno
ⓘ (0332) 624 136 ⓛ Villa 10.00–18.00 Wed–Sun, closed Mon &
Tues, Mar–Sept; 10.00–17.00 Wed–Sun, closed Mon & Tues, Oct–Feb.
Admission charge), a grand villa, set in a splendid baroque garden.

Locarno

The odd, curving shape of Locarno's central **Piazza Grande** follows
the original shoreline, before receding waters moved it away and
the space was paved with river stones to form the *piazza*. Behind are
twisted narrow streets, arcades and garden-filled courtyards with
medieval houses and fountains. Near the railway station, a funicular
takes passengers to **Orselina** for views and access to a *funivia* (cable
car) bound for higher **Cardada**. Locarno is the starting point for the
scenic Centovalli train excursion to Domodossola (ⓘ (91) 756 0400
ⓦ www.centovalli.ch). A major international event for film fans is the
Festival del Film di Locarno, when the main square, Piazza Grande
becomes a giant outdoor cinema each evening. This mid-August
event draws crowds from all over Europe, so be sure to book
lodgings early.

RETAIL THERAPY

Laveno is known for its ceramics, and several shops sell examples of it.
The museum **Civica Raccolta di Terraglia** (ⓐ Via Lungolago Perabo 1,
Cerro ⓘ (0332) 666 530 ⓛ 14.30–17.30 Tues–Thur, 10.00–12.00,
14.30–17.30 Fri–Sun, closed Mon, Sept–June; 14.30–17.30 Fri–Sun,
closed Mon–Thur, July & Aug. Admission charge) in the adjoining
village of Cerro is also devoted to ceramics.

Several towns have weekly markets, the largest of which is on
Wednesday in Luino. Smaller, but with somewhat better
merchandise, is the Saturday street market in Intra.

AFTER DARK

Nightlife in this region is more likely to involve a leisurely dinner on a romantic lakeside terrace than dancing until 04.00. But if you can't bear to leave your boogie boots at home, ask around and you should be able to locate a local spot with a DJ on Saturday night.

Restaurants

Trattoria Imbarcadero £ Metal bistro tables sprawl over a terrace, edging out into the lake. The Imbarcadero serves up local specials, including grilled lake fish. ⓐ Via Lungolago 12, Isola dei Pescatori ⓣ (0323) 30 329 ⓦ www.imbarcaderoisolapescatori.it ⓛ 12.30–14.30, 19.30–22.00 Apr–Oct, closed Nov–Mar

Monnalisa ££ Dine in sight of the lake on well-prepared traditional Italian dishes, with attentive staff and attractive décor. ⓐ Via Poli 18, Arona ⓣ (0322) 463 32 ⓛ 12.30–23.00

🔽 *Frescoes and a hearty fire in Locanda dei Mai Intees, Azzate*

Ristorante Belvedere ££ Nicely prepared fish and handmade pasta are served in a romantic vine-hung terrace overlooking the lake. ⓐ Via Piave 11, Ranco ⓣ (0331) 976 609 ⓛ 12.00–23.30 Mon–Sat, closed Sun

Il Sole di Ranco £££ One of northern Italy's finest restaurants, with two Michelin stars to prove it. Presentations and service are as outstanding as the creative dishes. ⓐ Piazza Venezia 5, Ranco ⓣ (0331) 97 6507 ⓦ www.ilsolediranco.it ⓛ 12.30–14.00, 19.30–21.00 Apr–Sept; 12.30–14.00, 19.30–21.00 Sat–Thur, closed Fri, Oct–Mar

Locanda dei Mai Intees £££ The chef-owned restaurant is set in a medieval manor house with priceless frescoes, but they pale in comparison to the delicate pastas and mains featuring locally grown ingredients. Well worth splurging. ⓐ Via Nobile Claudio Riva 2, Azzate (Varese) ⓣ (0332) 45 7223 ⓦ www.mai-intees.com ⓛ 12.00–23.00

Cinemas, music & theatres
All the larger lake towns have at least one cinema, although films will nearly always be in Italian. Several also have occasional free lakeside concerts and music events; local tourist offices will have schedules of these.

ACCOMMODATION
Albergo Verbano ££ A little gem on the charming Isola dei Pescatori. Staying here also means you can have a slice of this romantic island to yourself after the last daytrippers leave at 18.00. ⓐ Via Ugo Ara 2, Isola dei Pescatori ⓣ (0323) 331 29 ⓕ (0323) 331 29 ⓦ www.hotelverbano.it

ACROSS LAKE MAGGIORE

Only three boats a day run from Stresa and Verbania to Locarno, in Switzerland, but several more leave from Luino on the northeastern side of the lake. Or, at 09.45 a hydrofoil departs from Arona, arriving in Locarno at noon, and making a good scenic day trip. The easiest way to see the other towns in Swiss Maggiore is by bus no. 21 from Locarno, or to drive across the border. The crossing is usually fast. In either case, you will need your passport, since Switzerland is not a member of the EU.

Hotel Pironi ££ Vaulted ceilings and original frescoes set the scene at this 15th-century former palace. Wooden beams and antiques stud the reception and first-floor reading room, although the guest rooms are fairly modern. ⓐ Via Marconi 35, Cannobio ⓣ (0323) 70 624 ⓦ www.pironihotel.it

Piccolo Lago ££ This little *locanda* also has 12 rooms with balconies overlooking the lake and gardens. It's 5 km (3 miles) east of Verbania on the SP54. You have to cross the road to get to its lakeside pool. ⓐ Via Filippo Turati 87, Fondotoce ⓣ (0323) 586 792 ⓦ www.piccololago.it

---

❿ *Hop on one of the city's trams, the most convenient overland transport*

PRACTICAL
information

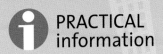

Directory

GETTING THERE
By air
Milan's Malpensa Airport is northern Italy's major air hub. Flights from within Europe often use the smaller Linate Airport.

From the UK and Europe
Ryanair (ℹ️ 899 678 910 🅦 www.ryanair.com) flies from Glasgow, Liverpool, Luton, Newcastle, Bournemouth, Bristol, East Midlands and Stansted to Bergamo's Orio al Serio Airport, often at ridiculously low fares. **Jet2** (ℹ️ 44 (0) 20 7170 0737 🅦 www.jet2.com) also flies to Bergamo from Leeds/Bradford, Manchester, Belfast and Edinburgh.

🔺 *Malpensa Airport is one of the two local international airports serving Milan*

EasyJet (☎ 848 887 766 ⓦ www.easyjet.com) serves Milan's central Linate Airport from Gatwick, plus Milan Malpensa from Bristol and Edinburgh. **FlyBe** (☎ 44 (0) 1392 268 529 ⓦ www.flybe.com) operates budget routes to Birmingham and Manchester. **British Airways** (☎ 199 712 266 ⓦ www.britishairways.com) has daily flights to both Milan's airports from Heathrow, with additional routes from Birmingham and Manchester to Malpensa. **Alitalia** (☎ 06 22 22 ⓦ www.alitalia.com) operates Heathrow to Malpensa and Linate routes.

From North America

There are direct flights from the USA from New York's JFK to Milan's Malpensa Airport on Alitalia (see above) and **Delta** (☎ 800 477 999 ⓦ www.delta.com), with a New York Newark route on **Continental** (☎ 026 963 3256 ⓦ www.continental.com).

From Australia and New Zealand

No direct flights are offered to any Italian city, so the best plan is to book the best price to a major European hub such as London or Frankfurt, with an onward connection to Milan.

Many people are aware that air travel emits CO_2 which contributes to climate change. You may be interested in the possibility of lessening the environmental impact of your flight through the charity Climate Care, which offsets your CO_2 by funding environmental projects around the world. Visit ⓦ www.climatecare.org

By rail

Milan's Stazione Centrale is on a direct rail link with Geneva and Paris, making the trip from London's St Pancras Station to Milan about ten hours. Less pricey are conventional trains. Travel time is about five hours from Paris by Eurostar, seven by slower train. Within Italy, be sure to stamp your ticket with the date at one of the yellow machines on the platform of the station before boarding.

Travellers from outside Europe who plan to use trains should investigate the various multi-day train passes on Trenitalia and multi-country travel offered by **Rail Europe** (☏ 44 (0)870 837 1371 ⓦ www.raileurope.com). For travellers anywhere, Rail Europe offers a one-stop source of information, reservations and tickets, including Eurostar. Also of use is the **Thomas Cook European Rail Timetable** (☏ (UK) 01733 416 477; (USA) 1 800 322 3834 ⓦ www.thomascookpublishing.com).

By road

The quickest way from London to Milan is via Reims and Basle along the E50, E25 and E35. This 1,200-km (750-mile) journey takes around 12 hours.

Although flying from the UK to Milan is relatively inexpensive, the London Victoria Coach Station to Milan trip on **Eurolines** (☏ 0870 514 3219 ⓦ www.eurolines.com) is also economical and takes around 24 hours.

ENTRY FORMALITIES

Citizens of Ireland, USA, Canada, New Zealand and Australia need only a valid passport to enter Italy and do not require visas for stays of up to 90 days. European citizens may stay without a visa for an unlimited period. Citizens of South Africa must have visas to enter Italy.

EU citizens can bring goods for personal use when arriving from another EU country, but must observe the limits on tobacco (800 cigarettes) and spirits (10 litres over 22 per cent alcohol, 90

litres of wine). Limits for non-EU nationals are 200 cigarettes, one
litre of spirits and two litres of wine.

MONEY

The euro (€) is the official currency in Italy. There are seven banknotes:
€5, €10, €20, €50, €100, €200 and €500. €1 = 100 cents. Coins are in
denominations of €1 and €2, and 1, 2, 5, 10, 20 and 50 cents. Currency
exchange facilities and cashpoints are available at Bergamo, Linate
and Malpensa Airports.

Both VISA and MasterCard are widely accepted in Italy; American
Express is often accepted as well. Many small hotels, *agriturismo*
(farm holiday) properties and small restaurants do not accept cards.
ATMs (*bancomat* in Italian) offer the best exchange rates, are found
even in small towns and never close. Ask your card issuer before
leaving home what network you can use in Italy and make sure that
your PIN number can be used abroad. If necessary, you can change
money at **Banca Ponti** (🅰 Piazza del Duomo 19 ☎ (02) 722 771
🕐 08.30–16.15 Mon–Fri, 09.10–12.45 Sat, closed Sun).

HEALTH, SAFETY & CRIME

Like in any large city, be aware of your surroundings and avoid
walking alone at night and in seedy neighbourhoods. Guard against
pickpockets by carrying only the cash you need. Report any thefts
immediately, and be sure to get a copy of the report (*denuncia*)
for insurance. There are different kinds of policemen, including
carabinieri, or national police, and *vigili*, or local officers. Both are
armed and can make arrests. You can report a crime to either, but
the paperwork must be completed at a *questura* (police station).

Although tap water is apparently safe, it's best to buy bottled
water if possible. Pharmacies are abundant (identified by a green

cross outside). Should you become ill or have an accident, medical care is very good and free to EU residents who obtain a European Health Insurance Card (EHIC) before leaving home. The website for ordering these cards is Ⓦ www.ehic.org.uk, and this card replaces the old E111 form. All visitors should carry travellers' health insurance if their own coverage does not cover reimbursement, and should also consider emergency medical evacuation insurance. Emergency treatment at hospitals is free to everyone.

Check the following websites for any additional information needed:

Travel & health advice for British citizens Ⓦ www.fco.gov.uk/travel, Ⓦ www.dh.gov.uk/travellers

Travel & health advice for American citizens Ⓦ www.cdc.gov/travel, Ⓦ www.healthfinder.com

World Health Organisation Ⓦ www.who.int/en

For police and medical emergency numbers, see Emergencies, page 152.

Pedestrians from left-hand drive countries need to be especially careful because traffic will be approaching from an unfamiliar direction. Motorcycles and scooters are very common, and you should always be aware of these approaching between vehicles or emerging suddenly from alleyways.

OPENING HOURS

Major attractions and museums are normally open 08.30 or 09.00 to 19.00 or 19.30 with Monday closing. Smaller ones may have shorter hours, frequently closing for lunch. Banks open 08.30–13.00 or 13.30, with an additional hour in the afternoon (approximately 15.00–16.00) Mon–Fri. Shops generally open 09.00 or 10.00 until 19.00 or 19.30 Mon–Sat, smaller ones with an hour or two closing at lunch and Monday morning closing. Sunday openings are becoming more common. Street markets open about 07.00 and close around midday. Pharmacies are usually open 08.00–13.00 and 16.00–20.00 Mon–Sat, and a sign on the door will direct you to the nearest one open Sundays and nights.

TOILETS

Public buildings, such as museums, usually have clean toilets in the publicly accessible areas near the entrance (or will let you in to use one in an emergency), and you will find occasional public facilities. But the fastest and easiest solution is to step into a bar or café and go directly to the back, following the sign 'toilet' or the universal symbols.

CHILDREN

Italians love children – and spoil them. In any small neighbourhood *trattoria*, your whole family will be welcomed and catered to. Hotels can usually provide cots free of charge (with advance notice), and you will rarely be charged for a child staying in a room with adults. Special infant needs, such as baby food and nappies, are available in supermarkets, but for a shorter stay it is often easier to bring familiar brands from home.

Although not every place is suitable for all ages, child-friendly sights in Milan include the Duomo roof (see page 60) and the natural history museum in Giardini Pubblici (see page 25). On a sunny day, head to the park behind Villa Reale, reserved exclusively for families with young children. Older children will enjoy the many working models in the Museo Nazionale della Scienza e della Tecnologia (see page 94) and the interactive exhibits there that allow them to perform scientific experiments. If you're heading out of town, castles are always a good bet, and there's a fine one as close as Angera (see page 130). Maggiore also has swinging cable cars to the mountaintop of Mottarone at Stresa (see page 122), and Como has a creaking funicular that climbs to Brunate (see page 115). Older kids will get a kick out of the quirky free transportation museum at Ranco (see page 131), where they can walk under the tracks to see how a funicular works and climb aboard trams and other vehicles.

COMMUNICATIONS

Internet

Internet is increasingly available, both in hotels and at internet cafés around the city. Most hotels now have in-room points or Wi-Fi. Tourist information offices and kiosks can provide lists of internet cafés and public access points such as libraries, or head to centrally located **FNAC** (❷ Via Torino ❶ (02) 869 541 ❸ 09.00–20.00 Mon–Sat, 10.00–20.00 Sun). Be sure to bring your passport, as ID is required.

Phone

All Milan numbers begin with 02, which must be dialled from inside or outside the city. Numbers can vary between six and nine digits, although most have eight. Numbers beginning with 800 are free. To use public telephones, buy a card (*scheda telefonica*) from a *tabacchaio* (tobacconist shop), designated by a capital white T on a black background. Hotel telephones usually carry a high surcharge, but not always, so ask at the desk.

Mobile phone numbers begin with 3; if you see an old number with the prefix 03, omit the zero. Your UK, New Zealand and Australian

❿ *Public transport comes in all shapes and sizes*

TELEPHONING ABROAD

To make an international call, dial 00, then the country code (UK = 44, Ireland = 353, US and Canada = 1, Australia = 61, New Zealand = 64, South Africa = 27) and number, omitting the initial zero in UK numbers.

TELEPHONING ITALY

To call Milan from abroad, dial 00 (from Europe), 011 (from the US) or 0011 (from Australia), followed by 39 (02) and the local number.

mobile phone will work in Italy; US and Canadian cell phones may not, so be sure to check with your provider before leaving home.

Post

For letters and postcards buy stamps (*francobolli*) at a *tabacchaio*; for special services go to a post office (*Poste e Telecommunicazioni*). Opening hours are 08.15–13.30 Mon–Fri, and until 12.30 Sat. If you pay extra for *posta priorità* (priority post), your mail should arrive the next day in Italy, within three days in the UK and about five days elsewhere. Post boxes are red, and are affixed to walls. They have two slots – one for letters within the city (*per la Città*), and one for all other destinations (*Altre Destinazioni*).

ELECTRICITY

Electrical current in Italy is 220V AC and plugs are two pin, round-pronged. British appliances will need a simple adaptor, easily obtained at any electrical or hardware store in Milan or at the airport during your travels. US and other equipment designed for 110v will need a transformer (*transformatore di corrente*).

TRAVELLERS WITH DISABILITIES

Milan is the happy exception to the enormous challenges much of Italy presents to those with limited mobility. Several of the city museums have disabled access, including Civico Museo di Arte Contemporanio, Galleria d'Arte Enrico, Museo Teatrale alla Scala and Palazzo Reale. Milan also has one of the best sites for information on access and assistance for travellers with disabilities ⓦ www.milanopertutti.it

Airport assistance: the Sala Amica provides assistance on check-in, boarding and disembarkation at both of Milan's major airports. This includes not only the loading process but waiting arrangements as well. Wheelchairs are carried free. Check-in is at the Sala Amica. Make arrangements to be met when booking your flight. ⓐ Malpensa Terminal 1 ⓣ (02) 5858 0298, ⓐ Malpensa Terminal 2 ⓣ (02) 5858 3266, ⓐ Linate ⓣ (02) 716 659

City transportation: Buses 39, 48, 49, 50, 54, 56, 57, 58, 65, 73, 78, 83, 84, 94 are fully accessible with low entry levels.

Access to trains: Look for the booklet *Servizi per la Clientela Disabile* at any railway station. It lists the stations with disabled reception centres (*Centro di Accoglienza Disabili*). For assistance at Stazione Centrale call ⓣ (02) 6707 0958. The ticket office and the waiting areas are accessible and the platforms are accessed by lift. It is a busy station, so allow extra time. Stazione Garibaldi (north- and west-bound trains) has a reception station for disabled travellers (ⓐ Centro di Accoglienza Disabili ⓣ (02) 6371 6105 or (02) 6371 6274). Ferovie Nord (Como and Varese) station at Via Cardona has accessible ticket offices and platforms. Some new, high-speed trains are accessed at platform level. Information and assistance can be arranged by calling ⓣ (02) 85 111 ⓦ www.ferrovienord.it

Elevator-equipped vans: make reservations at least 48 hours in advance to schedule the services of these taxi-vans equipped with wheelchair elevators.

Alatha ⓣ (02) 5796 41, Missione Handicap ⓣ (02) 4229 0549

CTA ⓣ (02) 3559 360, (02) 3574 768

Stella Cometa ⓣ (02) 8942 3078, (02) 8320 0752

In addition, useful organisations for advice and information before your travels include:

RADAR The principal UK forum for people with disabilities. ⓐ 12 City Forum, 250 City Road, London EC1V 8AF ⓣ (020) 7250 3222 ⓦ www.radar.org.uk

SATH (Society for Accessible Travel & Hospitality) advises US-based travellers with disabilities. ⓐ 347 Fifth Ave, Suite 605, New York, NY 10016 ⓣ (212) 447 7284 ⓦ www.sath.org

TOURIST INFORMATION

Tourist offices – Milan

IAT Tourist Reception and Information Offices The main office is in the Piazza del Duomo. ⓐ 19/A ⓣ (02) 3391 0794 ⓕ (02) 7740 4333 ⓦ www.milanoinfo.eu ◷ 08.45–13.00, 14.00–18.00 Mon–Sat, 09.00–13.00, 14.00–17.00 Sun

Information points – Milan

Stazione Centrale (Central Rail Station) ⓣ (02) 7740 4318 ◷ 08.00–19.00 Mon–Sat, 09.00–12.30, 13.30–18.00 Sun

Tourist offices – the lakes

IAT Como ⓐ Piazza Cavour 17, Como ⓣ (031) 269 712 ⓦ www.lakecomo.com ◷ 09.00–13.00, 14.30–18.00 Mon–Sat, closed Sun; 09.30–13.00 June–Sept ℹ A smaller kiosk is located on the south side of the Duomo

IAT Bellagio ⓐ Piazza Mazzini, Bellagio ☎ (031) 950 204 ⓦ www.bellagiolakecomo.com 🕐 09.00–12.00, 15.00–18.00 Mon–Sat, 09.00–12.00 Sun

IAT Tremezzo ⓐ Via Regina 3, Tremezzo ☎ (034) 440 493 ⓦ www.lakecomo.com 🕐 09.00–12.00, 15.30–18.30 Thur–Tues, Apr–Sept; closed Oct–Mar

Lake Maggiore Tourist Office ⓐ Via Principe Tomaso 70/72, Stresa ☎ (0323) 30 416 ⓦ www.illagomaggiore.com

Useful websites

ⓦ www.ciaomilano.it. A very useful site about Milan, with descriptions of museums and sights, restaurant and entertainment listings and helpful suggestions.

ⓦ www.enit.it. ENIT (The Italian Government Tourist Board) can also send you information packs about Milan and specialist holidays by direct request through their website.

BACKGROUND READING

The Last Supper: a Cosmic Drama and an Act of Redemption by Michael Ladwein. Art lovers will lap up this examination of the iconic painting's enduring legacy.

The Dark Heart of Italy by Tobias Jones. A penetrating gaze into the Italian psyche.

Art and Authority in Renaissance Milan by Evelyn Welch. A stunning study of the Sfroza and Visconti courts.

A History of Milan Under the Sforza by Cecilia Ady. Still in print after a century, this is a decade-by-decade run-through of Milan's wealthy Renaissance period.

Emergencies

The following are emergency freephone numbers:

Ambulance (*Ambulanza*) 🛈 118
Fire (*Vigili del Fuoco*) 🛈 115
Police (*Polizia*) English speaking helpline) 🛈 112

MEDICAL SERVICES

Should you become ill, you have several sources of information on English-speaking doctors. If you can reach your consulate, they can provide a list, or you can go prepared with the appropriate pages from the directory published by the International Association of Medical Assistance for travellers. **IAMAT** is a non-profit organisation that provides medical information on health-related travel issues all over the world, as well as a list of English speaking doctors (ⓦ www.iamat.org).

Accident and Emergency departments are open 24 hours, or call 🛈 118. This number will also provide you with the address of doctors on emergency call out. The following hospitals have A&E departments (*pronto soccorso*):

Ospedale Niguarda Ca' Granda ⓐ Piazza Ospedale Maggiore 3 🛈 (02) 6444 2381

Ospedale Gaetano Pini ⓐ Piazza Cardinal Ferrari 1 🛈 (02) 582 961

Ospedale dei Bambini (Children's Hospital) V Buzzi
ⓐ Via Castelvetro 32 🛈 (02) 5799 5363

There is a 24-hour pharmacy in Stazione Centrale (Ⓜ Metro: 2, 3), or call 🛈 800 801 185 to find out which pharmacies are open nearest to you.

▶ *Carabinieri stand guard in front of the Duomo*

Additional useful numbers:
Car breakdown ℹ 116

Lost or stolen credit cards:
American Express ℹ 800 864 046
Diners Club ℹ 800 864 064
MasterCard ℹ 800 868 068
VISA ℹ 800 821 001 (Americard), 800 877 233 (Eurocard)

POLICE

Should you need to report a theft (*furto*), missing person or any
other matter for the police, go to the *questura*, or police station.
If insurance is involved, be sure to obtain a copy of the *denuncia*,
a stamped form that you must have for filing claims.

Questura (Main Police Station) ⊕ Via Montebello 26 ℹ (02) 622 61,
English speaking (02) 863 701

To reach the police in an emergency, dial ℹ 112

EMERGENCY PHRASES

Help!	**Fire!**	**Stop!**
Aiuto!	Fuoco!	Fermi!
Ahyootoh!	*Fwohkoh!*	*Fehrmee!*

Call an ambulance/a doctor/the police/the fire service!
Chiami un'ambulanza/un medico/la polizia/i pompieri!
*Kyahmee oon ahmboolahntsa/oon mehdeecoh/
lah pohleetseeyah/ee pohmpyehree!*

Lost property

Oggetti Smarriti (City Lost and Found) ⓐ Via Fruili 30 ⓣ (02) 8845 3900 ⓒ 08.30-16.00 Mon–Fri ⓜ Metro: 3 to Porta Romana or Lodi; bus: 90, 91, 92

Central Railways Office ⓐ Via Sammartini 108 ⓣ (02) 6371 2667 ⓒ 07.00–13.00, 14.00–20.00 ⓜ Metro: 3 to Centrale; bus: 42, 81, 82, 90, 92; tram: 2, 9

EMBASSIES & CONSULATES

In general, it is a consulate that handles emergencies of travelling citizens, not the embassy. But if there is no consulate in a country, embassies take over these responsibilities. Your consulate or embassy should be the first place you turn to if a passport is lost, after reporting it to the police. Consulates can also provide lists of English-speaking doctors and dentists and can help you to find an English-speaking lawyer should you require one.

Australian Consulate ⓐ Via Borgogna 2 ⓣ (02) 777 0411 ⓕ (02) 7770 4242 ⓦ www.dfat.gov.au ⓜ Metro: 1 to San Babila

British Consulate ⓐ Via San Paolo 7 ⓣ (02) 723 001 ⓕ (02) 8646 5081 ⓦ www.britishembassy.gov.uk/italy ⓜ Metro: 1, 3 to Duomo

Canadian Embassy ⓐ Via Zara 30, Rome ⓣ (06) 854 441 ⓕ (06) 854 442 912 ⓦ www.canada.it

Irish Consulate ⓐ Piazza San Pietro in Gessate 2 ⓣ (02) 5518 7569 ⓕ (02) 5518 7570 ⓜ Bus: 60

New Zealand Consulate ⓐ Via Guido d'Arezzo 6 ⓣ (02) 499 0201 ⓕ (02) 4801 2577 ⓦ www.nzembassy.com ⓜ Metro: 1 to Pagano

South African Consulate ⓐ Vicolo San Giovanni sul Muro 4 ⓣ (02) 885 8581 ⓕ (02) 7201 1063 ⓦ www.sudafrica.it ⓜ Metro: 1 to Cairoli

US Consulate ⓐ Via Principe Amedeo 2/10 ⓣ (02) 290 351 ⓕ (02) 2900 1165 ⓦ www.usembassy.it/milan/cons ⓜ Metro: 3 to Turati

WHAT'S IN YOUR GUIDEBOOK?

Independent authors Impartial up-to-date information from our travel experts who meticulously source local knowledge.

Experience Thomas Cook's 165 years in the travel industry and guidebook publishing enriches every word with expertise you can trust.

Travel know-how Contributions by thousands of staff around the globe, each one living and breathing travel.

Editors Travel-publishing professionals, pulling everything together to craft a perfect blend of words, pictures, maps and design.

You, the traveller We deliver a practical, no-nonsense approach to information, geared to how you really use it.

Editorial/project management: Lisa Plumridge with Laetitia Clapton
Copy editor: Paul Hines
Layout/DTP: Alison Rayner
Proofreader: Wendy Janes

The publishers would like to thank the following individuals and organisations for supplying their copyright photographs for this book: Alcatraz Srl/Lorenzo Citterio, page 29; BigStockPhoto.com (Alessandro Bolis, page 31; Cheung Chi Man, page 153); The Chedi Milan, page 36; Dreamstime.com (Anshuca, page 84; BigPressPhoto, page 109; Gary718, page 66; lqsolution, page 61; Giorgio Micheletti, page 1; Joy Prescott, page 91; Margaret Smeaton, page 21); Peter Duhon, page 13; iStockphoto.com (Marc C. Fischer, page 62; Christopher Penler, page 113; Stefan Tordenmalm, pages 122–3); Locanda dei Mai Intees, page 136; Cristiano Maifre/SXC.hu, page 43; Alison Rayner, page 131; Kathryn Tomasetti, pages 17, 19 & 139; Charis Tsevis/SXC.hu, pages 40–1 & 140; Stillman Rogers, all others.

Send your thoughts to
books@thomascook.com

- Found a great bar, club, shop or must-see sight that we don't feature?
- Like to tip us off about any information that needs a little updating?
- Want to tell us what you love about this handy little guidebook and more importantly how we can make it even handier?

Then here's your chance to tell all! Send us ideas, discoveries and recommendations today and then look out for your valuable input in the next edition of this title.

Email the above address (stating the title) or write to:
CitySpots Project Editor, Thomas Cook Publishing, PO Box 227, Coningsby Road, Peterborough PE3 8SB, UK.